100
GREATS

TOTTENHAM HOTSPUR
FOOTBALL CLUB

STADIA

100
GREATS

TOTTENHAM HOTSPUR
FOOTBALL CLUB

ROY BRAZIER

This book is dedicated to the late Alan Rosenthal;
a long-term Tottenham Hotspur supporter, a gentleman
and a friend to many, of which I was privileged to be one.

First published 2006

STADIA is an imprint of
Tempus Publishing Limited
The Mill, Brimscombe Port,
Stroud, Gloucestershire, GL5 2QG
www.tempus-publishing.com

British Library Cataloguing in Publication Data.
A catalogue record for this book is available from the British Library.

ISBN 0 7524 3798 4

Typesetting and origination by Tempus Publishing Limited.
Printed in Great Britain.

Acknowledgements

Thanks once again to Nick Manning who helped me with various photographs from his large collection and also Andy Porter for his encouragement when I most needed it. Barry Young for all his help in putting the whole collection of the illustrations onto CD for me, while I would have spent many a long night trying to find out how this is done on my own. I should also like to thank Tempus themselves who gave me more time than I would have expected to finalise the book.

Introduction

With a book such as this, or indeed any kind of publication when players through the years are compared with each other, there are bound to be arguments as to who would be left out or who will be given a place. These legends of Tottenham Hotspur are simply my view of who constitutes a player who stood out above others while playing for the Spurs. What are the things to look for in such a publication? I decided at first on those who spent all or almost all of their careers at White Hart Lane, but this did not really work and so a long stay became the post from which to work. Then there were others who only performed a scattering of seasons but were still worthy of being included. Right from the beginning Tottenham Hotspur were a stylish team who drew large crowds when their pitch was on Tottenham marshes, and deep in the winters of the late 1890s the early players started the Spurs tradition of winning with flair. They moved to a ground of their own in Northumberland Avenue after other clubs on the marshes often took by force the Spurs pitch which was nearly always the better of muddy conditions. Tottenham had also attracted crowds in the thousands and an enclosed ground was the only way to continue. The spectators had been watching for free and they were now being asked to pay for their Saturday afternoon entertainment, but still the supporters came in great numbers. Aiming high, Spurs applied for admission to the Football League in 1896 but were not elected, so they joined the Southern League. After a spell when the cash slowed up a mite, they found that the site was not large enough so they moved to their present ground in the High Road in 1899, which was formerly a nursery. Tottenham had built a fine reputation for allowing their players to express themselves in the type of game they played, and soon they were attracting other young players; the type of fans who had become keen supporters and were being brought up to appreciate the Spurs style. Listing the legends of White Hart Lane, it was when the Spurs were winning trophies and applause that the best players were seen. The 1901 FA Cup winning team and the early years in the Football League gave us Morris, Cameron and Tait, plus V.J. Woodward, Steel and Darnell. The cup winners of 1921 came up with seven of the eleven being dubbed top players. So it continued in the same vein, but that is not to say the best players came in the Spurs' best teams. Arthur Rowe did not play in a top side nor win trophies as a player, but he did return to the club to be the manager of the 1950 and 1951 championship team. Bill Nicholson was another who became the manager of the double-winning side after being a playing member, and awarded an OBE. Altogether eight Spurs players were awarded the OBE or MBE, plus one knighthood, Sir Alf Ramsey. Throughout the sixties and seventies top players gushed forth from White Hart Lane, but slowly the long-serving player was disappearing from the scene, and only a handful are playing in the modern game. Money is now becoming more important than tying the players to just one club, and so legends are now very thin on the ground.

Tottenham Hotspur FC 100 Greats

Clive Allen
Paul Allen
Darren Anderton
Steve Archibald
Ossie Ardiles
Eddie Baily
Peter Baker
Philip Beal
Les Bennett
Danny Blanchflower
Bert Bliss
John Brooks
Vic Buckingham
Ron Burgess
John Cameron
Sol Campbell
Jimmy Cantrell
Stephen Carr
Martin Chivers
Harry Clarke
Tommy Clay
Ralph Coates
Alfie Conn
Jabez Darnell
Jimmy Dimmock
Ted Ditchburn
John Duncan
Len Duquemin
Terry Dyson
Justin Edinburgh
John Elkes
Mike England MBE
Ray Evans
Willie Evans

Mark Falco
Tony Galvin
Paul Gascoigne
A.H. 'Jack' Gibbons
Alan Gilzean
Jimmy Greaves
Arthur Grimsdell
Willie Hall
Tommy Harmer
Ron Henry
Glenn Hoddle
Mel Hopkins
David Howells
Chris Hughton
George Hunt
Pat Jennings MBE
Cliff Jones
Ledley King
Joe Kinnear
Jurgen Klinsmann
Cyril Knowles
Gary Lineker OBE
George Ludford
Gary Mabbutt MBE
Dave Mackay
Tony Marchi
Les Medley
Terry Medwin
Billy Minter
Tom Morris
John Morrison
Alan Mullery MBE
Jimmy Neighbour
Joe Nicholls

Bill Nicholson OBE
Maurice Norman
Eugene 'Taffy' O'Callaghan
Frank Osborne
Jimmy Pearce
Steve Perryman MBE
Martin Peters MBE
John Pratt
Sir Alf Ramsey
George Robb
Graham Roberts
Jimmy Robertson
Arthur Rowe
Frank Saul
Jimmy Seed
Teddy Sheringham
Bert Smith
Bobby Smith
Robert Steel
Sandy Tate
Peter Taylor
Erik Thorstvedt
Sid Tickridge
Ricardo Villa
Chris Waddle
Fred 'Fanny' Walden
Ian Walker
John Wallis
Bill 'Sonny' Walters
John White
Arthur Willis
Vivian Woodward

The twenty who appear here in italics occupy two pages instead of the usual one.

Clive Allen
Striker 1984-1988

	Appearances	Goals
League	97 (8)	60
FA Cup	11 (1)	9
League Cup	13 (1)	13
Europe	3 (1)	2
Other	32 (6)	28
TOTAL	173	

Clive is the son of Les Allen who was a member of the successful Spurs 1960s side. He was born in East London in May 1961, and was a prolific goalscorer from an early age for Essex Boys, London Schools and England Schools. He attracted scouts from all the London clubs, but after training at Spurs he decided to join Queens Park Rangers. Very soon Clive was playing for the England Youth and Under-21 sides, and after only one full season at Loftus Road, scoring 28 goals in 39 games, Arsenal paid £1.25 million for his services in June 1980. After playing three friendlies for them, he moved to Crystal Palace just a few weeks later for the same sum, and later completed the circle by moving back to Queens Park Rangers.

Tottenham then signed him from Loftus Road in August 1984, just after he made his full England debut in South America, as a substitute against Brazil. His first League match for Spurs saw him notch two goals against Everton in the opening game of the 1984/85 season, and he followed up with two more versus his former club Queens Park Rangers. He then suffered a series of injuries which very much limited his appearances for the next two seasons.

The arrival of David Pleat as manager at White Hart Lane coincided with a fully fit Clive Allen, and this produced a fantastic season for the forward in 1986/87. Wearing the no.7 shirt, he was played as a lone striker in the Spurs line-up, and set up a new goalscoring record for Spurs with 49 goals, adding another 7 in friendlies, in one season. He was well served by the Spurs midfield of Hoddle and Waddle, who made many openings for Clive Allen's clinical finishing. After scoring the opening goal in the FA Cup final against Coventry City, Clive was destined for the runners-up medal as Spurs lost 3-2, but he was voted Player of the Year by the Football Writers Association and the Professional Footballers Association.

Although he continued to score regularly, he could never revive his sparkling strike rate the next season and, despite bringing his England caps up to five, he moved from Tottenham to Bordeaux of France where he stayed just one year before returning to his native shores. He was on the roundabout once again with spells at Chelsea, West Ham United and his one English club outside London, Manchester City. He wound down his playing days with ultra-short periods at Colchester, Luton, Bristol City and Carlisle. He also spent time as an England Youth Coach and now looks after Spurs' reserve side. Clive's record at Spurs saw him score 112 goals in just under four years; not a bad average.

	Appearances	Goals
League	276 (16)	23
FA Cup	26 (1)	1
League Cup	42 (2)	4
Europe	6 (1)	0
Other	93 (7)	3
TOTAL	470	

Another member of the Allen family to be at White Hart Lane – Clive is his cousin and Les Allen his uncle. Before he arrived at Spurs, Paul had been the youngest player to play in an FA Cup final at Wembley, being just seventeen years and 256 days old when he played for West Ham in 1980 when they beat Arsenal 1-0. He had trained with Queens Park Rangers and Crystal Palace as a schoolboy but signed apprentice forms for West Ham United; he turned professional in August 1979, making his debut the next month.

After six seasons with West Ham, Paul joined Spurs in June 1985 for £400,000, a snip at today's inflated fees, and was a tireless midfield worker who, although not noted as a goalscorer, managed to turn up with some important ones during his Tottenham days. His best goal tally in a season was in 1989/90 when he registered eight goals. Though not really standing out in the Spurs XI, he was popular with his teammates and contributed much for the cause during his eight seasons at White Hart Lane.

He returned to Wembley in 1987 with Spurs, but had to be content with a losers' medal; however, he won a second FA Cup winners' medal in 1991, eleven years after his first with West Ham. He also played in two FA Charity Shield matches for Tottenham. Paul gained 33 caps for England Youth – a record – and also played three games with the England Under-21s.

His consistency was rewarded at the end of the 1988/89 season, when he was chosen to tour with the England 'B' party, but it was unfortunate that an injury robbed him of a well-merited place. He also had the responsibility of captaining the Tottenham side just once when Gary Mabbutt and Neil Ruddock were both absent; he carried out the task with his usual pride and seemed to be all over the pitch in the game against Everton in September 1992. Everyone knows who the goalscorers were in the 1991 FA Cup semi-final against Arsenal, but it was Paul Allen combining with Gascoigne which led to Lineker's second goal, while it was his jinking run which set up Paul Stewart's equaliser in the final against Nottingham Forest.

When Paul eventually left White Hart Lane it was a while before they could replace him with such industry. His last appearance in the Tottenham colours was at Sheffield United on 11 September 1993. Paul Allen left for Southampton later that month, and then played out his days training at Southend before joining Swindon.

Midfield 1992-2004

	Appearances	Goals
League	279 (26)	34
FA Cup	26 (2)	6
League Cup	30 (1)	8
Other	60 (9)	17
TOTAL	433	

Darren is Southampton-born but made his early mark in football at Portsmouth, joining their trainees in the summer of 1988 at sixteen years of age. He signed as a professional in February 1990 and made his senior debut in the same year against Cardiff City. Darren kept his place for the rest of that season for the south coast club, and was also beginning to attract some attention from several other higher league clubs. In Portsmouth's fine run in the FA Cup that year he played a starring role, scoring both goals in their victory over Leyton Orient, plus two more at Middlesbrough where they won 4-2. Facing Liverpool in the semi-final, Anderton gave his side the lead that seemed to be taking them to Wembley, only for a last-gasp equaliser by Liverpool which saw the dream fade.

Tottenham brought him to White Hart Lane in May 1992, for a reported fee of £1.75 million. With some of the Spurs' top players moving away, it was to Anderton they looked to pick up the midfield reins, but for a fairly inexperienced player it placed a lot on his shoulders. He struggled for a

period as he tried to settle down with Tottenham, and although he missed only a few games in his first season, he was carrying a niggling injury. An operation put things right and the next campaign saw Darren miss just one League match as he began to settle down and show much of why he had been brought to Tottenham.

He always looked a casual type of player but this was very deceptive, as vouched by defenders who were made to look slow when Anderton spurted past them with the ball seemingly tied to his bootlaces. He was soon selected for the England squad and was a success, either in laying off passes or spurting down the touchline, and became a regular member of the squad. Playing on the right side of midfield gave him just that little extra space and his searching crosses caused many problems for opposing defences, but just as he was enjoying life at White Hart Lane, along came another injury scare. This saw Darren miss quite a few games and in three seasons he struggled to keep fit, only appearing 39 times with just 7 goals to his name. Long spells in action were often tempered with a period on the sidelines, but he still played with confidence when fit and strong.

After twelve years at White Hart Lane he was the longest-serving player on the Spurs side, but with a change of manager in 2004 he was not retained and joined Birmingham City. When Glenn Hoddle took over at Wolverhampton Wanderers he quickly brought Anderton into the side in 2005. Darren joined Bournemouth in 2006. He had left behind at Spurs some good memories.

Steve Archibald
Striker 1980-1988

	Appearances	Goals
League	128 (3)	58
FA Cup	17 (1)	5
League Cup	18	7
Europe	22	8
Other	25 (2)	19
TOTAL	216	

Born in Glasgow in 1956, Steve started his football career with Scottish junior clubs Crofoot United and Fernhill Athletic, and at the age of eighteen was taken on as a part-time player with Clyde. He continued his job at Rolls Royce and was a member of Clyde's promotion winning team in 1978. Alex Ferguson saw his potential as a goalscorer and quickly snapped him up for Aberdeen at a cost of £25,000. Archibald then began his full-time career in football. Aberdeen had one of their best spells, reaching the Scottish Cup finals of 1979 and 1980 and winning the Scottish First Division in 1980. Archibald had already been noticed and selected for the Scotland Under-21 side, and as a substitute for the full Scotland team, making a goalscoring debut versus Portugal. Tottenham had tried various centre forwards since climbing back into the First Division, with no success, and the previous season had seen a midfield player heading the Spurs scoring list. Manager Keith Burkinshaw had been on the Archibald trail for a while before bringing him to White Hart Lane in May 1980 for a transfer fee of £800,000. He was a strong running player who was not afraid of taking on any type of defence, while his instinct and alertness when in the opponents' goalmouth saw him poach many goals from close in. He very soon cemented a firm and fruitful partnership with Spurs' other new acquisition Garth Crooks. In his first season

Steve Archibald missed only one game and was the club's top goalscorer with 25 goals. It was a successful season as Spurs were the 1981 FA Cup winners. Although not one of the heaviest players, Archibald was very deceptive as he held off mighty challenges with consummate ease and literally left many a defender floundering in his wake. The Spurs fans took him to their heart, and soon began to sing 'We'll take good care of you, Archibald' to the advert tune of British Airways. He led the Tottenham attack in the cup-winning sides of 1981 and 1982. Steve Archibald was a hat-trick hero on just one occasion, at home to Stoke City in the last match of the 1982/83 campaign. However Steve used to thrive in the Channel Islands whenever Spurs made out-of-season trips for friendlies; helping himself to 10 goals in 3 games in Jersey and Guernsey. With two midfield players of the calibre of Hoddle and Ardiles, Steve was the type of finisher following their defence-splitting moves. The only time that Archibald found goals hard to come by was in the European Cup, and in his 22 matches he only

Archibald always followed up any Spurs attack, looking for a slip from the goalkeeper. Not this time against Manchester City at White Hart Lane.

managed to get on the scoresheet 6 times. Following his initial good season at White Hart Lane, Steve found the going a bit tougher as injuries began to slow him down somewhat; he was missing from the line-up for 20 games and his goal contribution was just nine in one season. Whilst at White Hart Lane Archibald added 22 more caps for Scotland to his one whilst with Aberdeen. It was unfortunate that Steve fell out big time with manager Keith Burkinshaw just as he was probably approaching his best spell for Tottenham. Some point to a home match with Coventry City on 29 August 1983 when he insisted on coming off the field with an injury after Spurs had used up their substitutes. He did, however, miss the next four matches through injury, and was used as a sub for the game at Watford, before coming on to replace Gary Brooke and scoring the winning goal with a powerful drive from twenty-five yards. The relations between player and manager still proved quite strained, and his departure from Spurs came when Terry Venables signed him for Barcelona for £1.25 million While in Spain Archibald won the Spanish League and reached the European Cup final, plus four more caps for Scotland. Midway through the 1987/88 season he was allowed to leave Spain and returned to England, and Blackburn Rovers, on loan. Steve then had ten months at Hibernian before heading back to Spain for a spell with Espanol, returning to Scotland with St Mirren and Ayr United. His memory is still clear to the White Hart Lane faithful.

Ossie Ardiles
Midfield 1978-91

	Appearances	Goals
League	221 (16)	16
FA Cup	32	4
League Cup	31 (1)	3
Europe	8 (1)	2
Other	92 (14)	12
TOTAL	416	

Ossie was the first footballer from South America to make a real success in Britain, and opened up a completely new chapter in Football League history. Born in 1952, Ossie first played for Red Star Cordoba (Argentina), his home-town club, and later moved to Huracan, where he stayed for eight seasons. He won his first international cap in 1976 while on a tour of Europe. When the 1978 World Cup was won by Argentina, the host country, one of the shining stars was Ossie Ardiles. As the rest of the world watched, Spurs manager Keith Burkinshaw stepped in to bring him to White Hart Lane, together with his international teammate Ricardo Villa, for a combined sum of £325,000.

Ardiles made his debut for Tottenham in a pre-season friendly against Royal Antwerp in Belgium. Everybody, it seemed, wanted to see Tottenham's two new stars; the first League match at Nottingham Forest brought in a crowd of 41,223, well above average. A rude awakening waited for Ardiles in his fourth game when Liverpool beat Spurs 7-0 at Anfield. It was Spurs' first season back in the First Division after a year in the Second Division and they finished in mid-table, with Ardiles missing only six games. He was absent just three times the following season, showing he had adapted well to the British game. Some thought his small frame would suffer but he was quick as well as an artist, and could sidestep hard tackles.

Ossie's dream, however, was to play at Wembley with 'Tott-ing-ham', and this came true when they won the FA Cup in 1981, beating Manchester City after a replay. Although Spurs were a pleasure to watch, especially with the diminutive Argentine pulling the strings, their only successes seemed to be in the cup matches. During Ossie's spell at Tottenham they could not reach the top of the First Division; they were in third place twice and fourth spot in two other seasons. The FA Cup final was reached for the second time in 1982, facing fellow London rivals Queens Park Rangers. Ardiles was not just a football brain; he was a qualified lawyer, and seemed to conduct himself with all the dignity of that profession. Many fans saw him much like old favourite Blanchflower in the way that many moves started in the mind of this midfield maestro, and he always played his heart out for Spurs.

Preparations for the World Cup of 1982 saw Ardiles return to Argentina to join their squad, but it was thought that he would be able to play in the FA Cup final. The Falklands conflict came along and Ossie, whose two young boys,

Ardiles kept a tight contol of the ball, looking for an opening. He is shown here in the all-white Spurs colours of 1986/87, and sporting a moustache, which he later discarded.

Pablo and Federico, had been born in England, was torn between two homes. Spurs loaned him to French club Paris St Germain. Following a quick return from his exile to White Hart Lane he picked up some niggling injuries, robbing him of his high standards. These slowed him down and tackles were catching him more often; he was never the same as he was in his early days at Tottenham. In only his fourth game back in a Tottenham shirt he had the misfortune to break a bone in his leg at Maine Road, resulting in ten months of inactivity before he was back playing again. His appearances stuttered from then on, and he was only on the bench for the UEFA Cup final versus Anderlecht in 1984. This went Spurs' way after a penalty shoot-out, and after receiving his winners' medal Ossie went to Steve Perryman, the Tottenham captain who missed out in the final, and handed it to him.

Ardiles was granted a benefit match in May 1986 when Inter Milan came to White Hart Lane. But more was to come and he was back at Wembley in 1987, Spurs losing to Coventry City, the first defeat for Tottenham in a major cup final. In August he played as substitute for the Football League against the Rest of the World in a centenary match, then captained the Football League side versus the Irish League. Ardiles joined Blackburn Rovers on loan during the 1987/88 season in their promotion drive, then joined Queens Park Rangers, but a second broken leg restricted his appearances. He went into management at Swindon Town, with spells in charge at Newcastle and West Bromwich Albion, and also in Japan, before returning to Tottenham as manager. His flamboyant style made each game exciting, but he left the post after less than two years. He is now back home in Argentina in a coaching position.

	Appearances	Goals
League	297	64
FA Cup	29	5
Other	56	21
TOTAL	382	

After spending eleven years at White Hart Lane as a player, Eddie returned later as assistant manager to Bill Nicholson, and, although two different characters, they were at the helm for a successful period of Spurs history. As an inside forward, Baily started his Tottenham career with the juniors and Finchley, and then during the Second World War as an amateur. During his army service he had plenty of experience turning out for the British Army against other service teams.

Baily was still in the unpaid ranks when he made his debut in the Football League versus West Bromwich Albion on 4 January 1947. His sense of humour led to his nickname of the 'Cheeky Chappie', with not a dull moment in the dressing room. For all his tricks, he was a vital cog in the Spurs line-up in the early 1950s. Three England 'B' matches were followed by a full England cap against Spain in Rio de Janeiro during the 1950 World Cup. Baily went on to play for his country nine times, with a goal in each of his first five matches. Some said he was worth his inclusion just to keep the international XI on their toes, but it was his football skill that really stood out. He also played for the Rest of the United Kingdom team versus Wales; five times for the Football League; and, as late as 1957, in an England side against Young England when thirty-two years of age.

With Les Medley at outside left, he formed one of the most entertaining partnerships in Spurs' history, and this was recognised by England as well, when the pair were selected together in four England matches. Arthur Rowe's team of 'push and run' was shown to perfection as Baily and Medley moved across the White Hart Lane mud exchanging passes in bewildering style. In January 1956, Baily, still a regular in the Tottenham XI, having missed just one match the season before, left Tottenham after 382 appearances and 90 goals. Eddie played his last game in a Spurs shirt at Burnley on 17 December 1955.

He moved to Port Vale for a £6,000 fee, where he stayed for only nine months before joining Nottingham Forest. He helped them gain promotion from the Second Division before coming back to London and Leyton Orient, where he finished his playing career then joined the coaching staff. In October 1963 Baily came home to White Hart Lane and became assistant manager to Bill Nicholson, holding that position for eleven years and leaving when Nicholson stood down as manager in 1974. He spent a few years as a scout for West Ham.

Peter Baker

Right-back 1952-1965

	Appearances	Goals
League	299	3
FA Cup	27	0
Europe	16	0
Other	58 (2)	0
TOTAL	402	

One of the most underrated members of the Tottenham Hotspur double-winning team of 1960/61, London-born Baker came to the notice of Spurs while playing for Enfield, and was signed on amateur forms in June 1949. He was with the club until May 1965, a period of just a fraction under sixteen years. Baker was already a youth international with England, and continued playing for Enfield for three more years as a Spurs amateur before turning professional at Tottenham. He then made his debut in a 1-1 draw at Sunderland in April 1953; regular right-back Alf Ramsey was on England duty, and further appearances also came when Ramsey was unavailable. He learnt much from the future England manager and, when he retired, Peter looked to be the one to follow in his footsteps. To his credit he fought for his place in the Tottenham XI and eventually claimed his spot at no.2 early in the 1956/57 season, missing only four League games.

For a full-back, Baker was extremely fast; he had to be, playing behind the efficient

Blanchflower, who got carried away at times with his attacking forays. Baker's style of play was not extravagant and, although he could be quite strong in the tackle, he always seemed to favour keeping his opponents away from the Spurs' goal and danger zone. He also kept his passes simple and mainly short, but would then surprise everyone with a defence-splitting through ball.

Although Peter was not selected for the full England squad – not being able to displace Jimmy Armfield from the national XI – he made his place in Tottenham's great team of the early sixties his very own. He was one of the unheralded stars of the Spurs' victory over Leicester City when the FA Cup final gave them the first ever 'double' of the twentieth century. With the arrival of Cyril Knowles at White Hart Lane, thirty-four-year-old Baker's position was becoming hard to hold onto, and he played only three games in the 1964/65 season. In May 1965 he left Tottenham, after chalking up 402 appearances and 3 goals against his name, and emigrated to South Africa, playing for Durban United and later becoming their manager. He also coached another Durban-based team, Abbinton, and settled down in South Africa, where he also made a very successful business career.

Philip Beal
Defender 1960-1965

	Appearances	Goals
League	330 (3)	1
FA Cup	30	0
League Cup	27	0
Europe	30	0
Other	62 (1)	0
TOTAL	483	

Beal was one of the few players to spend most of his playing career with one club. His first match was in 1963 when all the greats of the 'double' side were still at the club; Beal was at right half for Blanchflower. His last was the all-important final match of the season against Leeds United on 28 April 1975; Tottenham had to win to avoid relegation, which they did 4-2. Beal spent fifteen years at the club, becoming one of the longest-serving players for Spurs.

Phil started out with Surrey Schoolboys and was spotted by a Tottenham scout in their match versus Kent at Charlton. He had decided to make a career in the Merchant Navy before he received a letter inviting him to White Hart Lane for a trial. He then signed amateur forms for Spurs in 1960 at the age of fifteen, turning professional two years later. He had quite long spells in various defensive positions, his best season being 1973/74, Bill Nicholson's last full season as manager, when he missed just 1 match out of 44. Beal had to wait until his 138th game to score his one and only goal, which came in a 3-2 win over Queens Park Rangers at White Hart Lane on 29 January 1969. It was a goal to remember as he burst out of defence and ran eighty yards then played a neat one-two with Greaves and drove the ball hard into the opponents' net.

When Mullery arrived at Tottenham in 1964, Beal seemed to be the player to be left out, but his versatility meant he could perform with distinction in any midfield or defensive position. He was soon back in the Spurs line-up at right-back, after Norman suffered a serious injury, and had a lengthy spell in the no.2 shirt. His fellow professionals acclaimed him after a fine performance in the Football League Cup final victory against Aston Villa in 1971, and he went on to pick up another League Cup medal and a UEFA Cup winners' medal in 1972. However, a broken arm kept him on the sidelines and he had to sit and watch the 1967 Chelsea versus Tottenham FA Cup final. When MacKay left Spurs, the man turned to was Phil Beal, and a long run in the team saw him given a man-marking assignment in several matches; a job he was well suited to. He finally left White Hart Lane for Brighton, and then came spells in America with Los Angeles and Memphis. He returned to his homeland and, after just a few games with Crewe Alexandra, he retired.

	Appearances	Goals
League	273	104
FA Cup	22	14
Wartime	26	8
Other	57	44
TOTAL	378	

Born in Wood Green, Les was just starting out in his football career when the Second World War came along to interrupt everything. He had shone while playing for Wood Green, Middlesex and London Schools, and was still at school when he was in Spurs Juniors, and the usual spell at Northfleet. The eleventh game of the wartime matches produced the headline 'Wood Green Youth Shines'; Bennett had scored a hat-trick in his first senior outing, and Spurs had beaten Watford 8-2. Eleven appearances and seven goals were young Bennett's total at the end of the first wartime season.

He played only a few games for Tottenham during the war, but kept his eye in as a guest with Torquay, and then at Distillery, where he represented the Northern Ireland League versus the League of Ireland. Spending time overseas, Les continued to play when he could in Egypt, India and Burma, and was a member of the famous Dennis Compton side which toured the East.

When demobbed, he was included in the Tottenham line-up at inside right straight away, with much expected of him, as a skilful player who played in the traditional Spurs way. He was now twenty-eight, but was still an important part of the Tottenham side which captured the Second Division title and the First Division title in successive seasons (1950 and '51). Being such a good ball player, it was sometimes said that in the 'push and run' side Les could be given the ball when a rest was needed and he would dribble around for a while. Two other inside forwards were brought to White Hart Lane at this time, Rees and Murphy, but Les Bennett kept them on the sidelines and they soon moved on.

He never gained international recognition but was selected for the FA XI against the Army, Navy and Oxford University in the late 1940s. Aged thirty-six, Les was allowed to move to West Ham United early in the 1954/55 season following John Brooks' transfer to Tottenham from Reading. Les spent only one season at West Ham, which included a spell as captain, before he joined non-League Romford. He wound down his football career at Clacton Town as their manager. In his Tottenham days he scored 170 goals in a grand total of 378 appearances.

Danny Blanchflower
Wing half 1954-1964

	Appearances	Goals
League	337	15
FA Cup	33	4
League Cup	12	2
Other	54 (1)	26
TOTAL	437	

One of the most famous and popular players in Spurs' history, he was his own man throughout his career, on and off the field. Indeed it could be said that one of his most memorable moments came off the field when he refused to be the subject of TV's *This Is Your Life* programme.

His long and illustrious career began with Glentoran in Northern Ireland in 1945. Born in Belfast on 10 February 1926, Danny went on to become one of the household names of modern-day soccer. In the late 1930s, together with his brother Jackie, who went on to play for Manchester United, he honed his skills by playing with a tennis ball in the streets. Come the war and Danny volunteered for the RAF in 1944. He played one game for Swindon Town during the war, plus several games with their reserves, and was in Canada when the conflict ended.

Danny signed as a professional for Glentoran at £3 a week, and was soon selected for the Irish League XI. In 1948 he came to England, when Angus Seed at Barnsley paid £6,500 for his services, and his first cap for Northern Ireland quickly followed this in 1949. His debut was against Scotland at Windsor Park, but they lost 8-2. From then on Danny was a regular in the international team, and captain in most of the 56 matches he played. Danny parted company with Barnsley in March 1951 and moved to Aston Villa for £15,000, but soon learned they were living on their past glories. One of his first goals came in a game versus Spurs.

A transfer request saw him arrive at White Hart Lane in 1954, where player and club approved of the same style and cultured ways. Blanchflower came to Tottenham to replace the ageing Bill Nicholson and it was through the pairing of these two brains that Spurs had probably the best spell in their history. The fee of £30,000 proved to be the finest investment the north London club ever made. The Spurs' fine side of the early fifties was breaking up and it was around Danny that the new team was based. Arthur Rowe was still manager at that time and within a year Danny was in place as captain. But, when Rowe stepped down, Blanchflower was frustrated in his efforts to be a captain who had

Seen here receiving the FA Cup, Blanchflower led Spurs to cup wins in 1961 and 1962.

control on the field and not just the one who led the team out and spun the coin. In the 1958/59 season he asked for a transfer, but as luck would have it Bill Nicholson was appointed manager in March 1959; he quickly gave the captaincy back to Danny and began to build a Tottenham side to challenge for honours.

For many football admirers, the Spurs team of 1960 to 1963 was the most cultured League side they had ever seen, with Danny in its midst. He was Footballer of the Year in 1958, and again in 1961. Nicholson and Blanchflower did collide sometimes but generally they worked together for the good of Tottenham Hotspur. Danny was much more than just a great footballer, and being a typical Irishman had the right answer for most things; some of the tales are retold again and again. Blanchflower led Spurs to the double, the FA Cup twice and the European Cup-Winners' Cup. Danny often told of telling Mr Fred Bearman, the Tottenham chairman at the beginning of the 1960/61 season, that Spurs would win the double.

Although arriving at White Hart Lane at twenty-eight years of age, he often outshone younger players, and a lasting memory is of a smiling mud-stained face after being brought down headfirst in the Spurs mud of those times. He was a player who wanted to play and, even in the heat of battle, Danny would be calling for the ball; when he received it he promptly imposed his presence on the game, with every Spurs player responding to his captaincy.

A knee injury had been troubling him for a while and so he made the decision to retire while still playing at the top of the tree. He then made himself a further career in journalism, penning many a controversial line or two in his Fleet Street articles. Everyone knows that Blanchflower was the person that Bill Nicholson wanted to succeed him as manager at Spurs, but unfortunately this never materialised. He had a short spell as manager at Chelsea but found that this side of the game was not for him. Those who saw Danny Blanchflower in action close their eyes and still see him playing at his peak.

Bert Bliss
Inside forward 1911-1923

	Appearances	Goals
League	195	91
FA Cup	21	13
Wartime	64	44
Other	35 (1)	20
TOTAL	316	

Born in Staffordshire in March 1890, Bliss was spotted by Tottenham playing for Birmingham Juniors. He had started out with his home-town team Willenhall Swifts, and Spurs moved quickly to sign him on in April 1912. When taking him to London, Spurs made a gift of £50 to his club. Standing at only 5ft 6ins and ten stone, it was not for his powerful physique that he was brought to White Hart Lane: it was his terrific shooting power which stood him out from other forwards. In his first full season at Tottenham, 1914/15, his shoot-on-sight policy gave him 23 goals in all matches. Unfortunately Spurs finished at the bottom of the table that year, winning only 8 league matches and losing 18. Bert Bliss also went on to a 'grand tour' of Europe with Spurs in 1912, which took in Belgium, Germany, Austria and Hungary, playing eight games in twenty days. Tottenham and Bliss also returned to Germany, Italy and Switzerland in 1914, just before the outbreak of war, for an itinerary of nine games in twenty-four days.

He was often looked upon as one of the most deadly shots in football, even after making allowances for the ones which landed in the terraces. Bliss made his debut at home against Manchester City on 8 April 1912, and played in the last five games of the season, taking the place of Bob Steel, at inside left, who was retiring. It was this position that Bliss made his own, and he had only one short spell at no.8, plus one appearance at centre forward during the First World War. Throughout the first years of the war he managed to play quite regularly, but in the last two wartime seasons he could only manage four appearances. He more than made up for this by being an ever-present in 1919/20, top-scoring with 33 goals as Tottenham won the Second Division in style. He was yet another player who probably lost most of his best years to the 1914-1918 conflict.

Bert Bliss played his last game for Spurs on 4 November 1922 versus Liverpool. He moved just up the road to Clapton Orient, and retired after a season at Bournemouth & Boscombe Athletic. In his twelve years at Tottenham, Bliss scored 168 goals and made 316 appearances; not a bad average. He also played once for England, against Scotland, in 1921, making up the England left-wing triangle with Grimsdell and Dimmock.

John Brooks

Inside forward 1953-1960

	Appearances	Goals
League	166	46
FA Cup	13	5
Other	43	21
TOTAL	222	

A very skilful inside forward who was born in Reading, John Brooks joined the apprentice ranks of his home-town club after playing for Reading and Berkshire Schools. After just six weeks he signed professional forms and was quickly in the First XI of Reading. He joined Tottenham from Reading in February 1953, and was looked upon as a player in the typical Spurs style. Two players moved to Reading as part of the deal: Dennis Uphill, who had only eight appearances to his name, and Harry Robshaw, with just three games in the Spurs First XI, plus £3,000. John made his debut in a 2-0 defeat at Stoke City in April of the same year. He struggled for a time to pick up the rhythm of the First Division, and shared the inside forward berth with the long-serving Les Bennett in his first full season at White Lane, playing 18 games. When Bennett moved to West Ham in 1954 John settled into the team with ease, and soon he was showing all the skill and aptitude he had promised. He was slightly unlucky as he was at White Hart Lane in the spell between the 'push and run' and the 'double' eras, but he was spotted by the England selectors and capped versus Wales in November 1956. He only played three times for England, scoring in two of the three games, but with Johnny Haynes being of the same style as Brooks there was not room for both, and the game against Denmark was the last for his country. Although a regular for Tottenham in the mid-fifties, Brooks in full flow was a rare sight; he was never a consistent performer and at times he didn't show enough determination. As a result he never lived up to his potential. Approaching the 1960s, he was dropped at times and he appeared at outside left in his last game for Spurs at Luton on 14 November 1959. Brooks left Tottenham in the same way he joined, transferring to Chelsea as part of a £20,000 deal which saw Les Allen move in the opposite direction in December 1959. The Stamford Bridge team was fighting relegation fears and Brooks helped to prevent this happening. Two years later he moved down the road to Brentford, then finished his League career with three seasons at Crystal Palace before moving into non-League circles. Spells at Stevenage and Cambridge City preceded two summers in Toronto, Canada. He last spell was as player-manager with Knebworth. He always kept quite fit and was still making the odd appearance when nearly sixty. In his 222 matches for Tottenham he scored 72 goals.

Vic Buckingham
Defender 1935-1949

	Appearances	Goals
League	208	1
FA Cup	26	0
Wartime	61	1
Other	16	0
TOTAL	311	

Vic was born in Greenwich, south London in 1915 but made his mark in the north of the capital. Spotted when quite young, he started on his long Tottenham career with Spurs Juniors and was also selected for English Schools, before signing amateur forms at White Hart Lane at sixteen years of age. Like many young Spurs players at that time he was sent to Northfleet, the nursery club of Tottenham, linking up with George Ludford, Bill Whatley and Arthur Hitchins, some of the other Spurs juniors at the Kent club.

Nearly six feet in height, Vic was always a stylish player and spent almost all his games at Tottenham either at full-back or wing half. He made his debut at centre half in the senior team against Bury on 16 November 1935, filling in for Rowe who was injured, and made 16 appearances in the Spurs XI, who were back in the Second Division after a very short period in the First Division. In the 1938/39 season Buckingham missed only one match, settling down at left half. Then came the war and, although he was in the team that started the season, he was restricted from appearing for his parent club for long periods of the war. As a PT Instructor in the RAF, Vic moved around and played as a guest for Fulham, Millwall, Portsmouth, and Crewe Alexandra. It was while playing for Portsmouth that he found himself appearing for the naval town against Tottenham one Saturday. During the war Vic was selected twice for the England side versus Wales, and many representative games with the

FA XI and RAF teams. Altogether Buckingham played 311 times for Spurs, from 1935 until his last appearance versus Cardiff City on 5 March 1949, scoring just two goals. All his games were in the Second Division.

Vic turned to coaching after his retirement and had already coached in Norway in the summer of 1946, so he took over Spurs Juniors and at the same time coached Oxford University and Pegasus, who won the FA Amateur Cup in 1951. He was then manager of Bradford Park Avenue, West Bromwich Albion, who won the FA Cup and finished second in the First Division, and then took a coaching post for Ajax of Amsterdam in 1959. His services were widely acclaimed and he returned to England to take charge at Sheffield Wednesday and Fulham, but returned to the Continent to the managers' chair at Ethnikos of Greece and then Seville in Spain. Vic was well known for his managerial and coaching skills as well as his playing at Tottenham.

	Appearances	Goals
League	301	16
FA Cup	27	1
Wartime	131	43
Other	49	5
TOTAL	508	

One of the greatest players to wear the white shirt of Tottenham with pride, and a player whom manager Arthur Rowe once said was the finest post-war wing half in the country; irreplaceable in any team. Born in South Wales in 1917, Ron was a member of the Ebbw Vale Schools team and on leaving school joined his home team Cym Villa; it was then that a football scout for Tottenham Hotspur spotted him. He had been promised a trial by Cardiff City but had heard nothing so he was working as a pit boy. Arriving at Tottenham from the Rhondda Valley in May 1936 he signed amateur forms for the club. He worked on the ground staff as a junior; painting and sweeping, training in the evenings, and joining in the weekly practice match. Ron was a forward in the early days and after a year he was told that he would not make the grade, and was to be released. Before he left he went to the ground to watch the Tottenham 'A' side play and as luck would have it they found themselves a player short. Ron quickly put on a shirt to make up the XI at half-back where he had not often played, but he gave it a go. He did this so well that the club did not let him leave and gave him a rise to £3 a week and a place at their nursery side at Northfleet, where an ever-increasing group of Spurs youngsters were farmed out from Tottenham.

It was halfway through the 1938/39 season that Ron played his first match for Spurs, on 4 February 1939 at home to Norwich City, at right half, and he held his place for the rest of the season. He also played one game at inside left, where he had first impressed Tottenham. His first goal came, however, versus Swansea towards the end of the season. Ron's career was interrupted by the war but he played many games for Spurs during those dark days, a great deal of them as a forward, and scored 43 goals. In the RAF he played as a guest for Nottingham Forest, Notts County, Reading and Millwall, plus nearly 30 games for the RAF, Combined Forces, and FA teams, and was picked for Wales 12 times, although these wartime matches did not count as official internationals.

Ron Burgess and Stan Matthews. Two football legends come together in the 1948 FA Cup semi-final at Villa Park.

He soon made his full debut for his country and went on to win 32 caps, captaining Wales numerous times between 1946 and 1954. Ron was the first Welshman to play for the Football League XI, and for Great Britain versus the Rest of Europe at Hampden Park in 1947. Resuming after the war, Ron Burgess settled down at no.6 for Spurs and was made captain, a roll in which he prospered and led by example with his surging runs from well inside his own half of the field. He was recognised as one of the finest attacking wing halves known in the game.

As an inspiring leader he led Tottenham Hotspur to one of the best spells in their history. Under manager Arthur Rowe, Spurs won the Second Division and the First Division championships in successive years, between 1949 and 1951, in what became known as the 'push and run' era; 'make it simple, make it quick' was another way in which Spurs' distinctive style of football was known. It was a time when a group of players under an inspiring captain and manager became one of the best outfits in the history of football. To watch this fine side perform each week at a faster than fast rate was sublime itself, and Ron revelled in the role he played. If some tough tackling was needed he was on hand to take the game by the scruff of the neck and remind the team of what playing the Spurs way was all about.

Tottenham never had such a tireless worker, as he ranged the pitch tirelessly in every game, some saying he ran a marathon each week on what were then some very soggy football pitches. He gave almost all his football life to the club for fifteen seasons. It was in May 1954 that Burgess left Tottenham to take the post of player-manager at Swansea, and later just manager, before moving to Watford four years later as manager. Short spells at Hendon, Bedford and Fulham followed before he retired from football.

John Cameron

Inside forward 1898-1907

	Appearances	Goals
S. League	118	43
W. League	33	16
FA Cup	25	7
Other	118	73
TOTAL	294	

With a new century approaching, John Cameron joined Tottenham Hotspur in the autumn of 1898. After starting his football-ing career with Ayr Parkhouse, his local team, he moved to Queen's Park, the all-amateur club, and was soon representing Scotland. He then came south to England, playing for Everton, still as an amateur, and working for the Cunard Shipping Company. It was Frank Bettell, Spurs' first manager, who brought the classy goalscor-ing inside forward to north London, and it was a major signing in Spurs' history.

Cameron, more than anyone at the time, shaped the club into the traditional, elegant and stylish outfit that Tottenham have been ever since. Tottenham were members of three differ-ent leagues, also competing in the FA Cup, and in Cameron's first season they finished in third place in all three, with their new player from north of the border weighing in with 33 goals. He had now joined the professional ranks and, just a month into the season, Bettell resigned. John Cameron, a conscientious worker, took on the post of player-manager-secretary and also secretary of the fairly new Players and Trainers Union. During the summer of 1899 he signed six new players, including three more from Scotland, choosing his players with care and blending experience with ambition. This strengthened the side to such an extent that they became champi-ons of the Southern League in 1899/1900, and were unbeaten at home. Matches were won 7-0 over Thames Ironworks and 6-1 against Cowes and Brighton, with Cameron still scoring regu-larly, his total being 23 goals. He disliked 'rough play and rough manners' and believed a player must also have the qualities of a fine character combined with education.

In 1901 the Cameron handpicked team won the FA Cup against Sheffield United, a strong team with more experience than Spurs, who were a non-League team at the time. At a celebration dinner John Cameron met with an enthusiastic reception when he rose to make a modest speech, in which he praised the players in bonding quickly a team which made the win-ning of the FA Cup such an accomplishment. In 1906 he was reinstated as an amateur and gave up the secretary post, and then in March 1907 he resigned as manager and player. When in 1914 the war broke out, he was in Germany as a coach and was interned for a while. Afterwards he had a short spell as manager of Ayr United before becoming a sports journalist.

	Appearances	Goals
League	246 (9)	10
FA Cup	28 (2)	1
League Cup	28	4
Europe	2	0
Other	39 (11)	3
TOTAL	365	

Campbell was one of the most successful players to be home-grown by Tottenham Hotspur, whom he joined as a trainee straight from school, although he confessed to supporting Arsenal as a small boy. He was born in Newham on 18 September 1974 and attended Idsall School in Shifnal. He went on to represent Newham School, before being signed up by Spurs. Sol joined Spurs' trainee staff in the summer of 1991 after being one of the five graduates from Tottenham to make the grade from the School of Excellence at Lilleshall. In his first full season at White Hart Lane he made 7 appearances in the junior side, notching 3 goals. Spurs' youth team coach Pat Holland picked him out as he said 'I was very pleased with him and I think he is going to be a good player.'

Campbell was a member of a strong Spurs youth side who in 1992/93 completed the double of the South East Counties championship and the League KO Cup, with three of the team making appearances in the League side. Early in his career at White Hart Lane Sol was looked upon as a midfield player, until he moved into the defensive role in which he starred. He won eleven caps for the England Under-21s, and nine England Youth caps. He made his Spurs debut coming on as substitute in a home game

with Chelsea in December 1992, marking the occasion with a goal, and he then settled in the line-up the next season with 42 appearances and again 1 goal (in the Coca-Cola Cup).

He was the obvious choice to take over from Gary Mabbutt as captain of Tottenham when he retired in the summer of 1998. It was Sol who lifted the Worthington (Football League) Cup at the end of the 1998/99 season when George Graham was Spurs' boss. Campbell had also cemented his place in the full England team by this time. Goals also came Campbell's way, mainly when advancing upfield for free-kicks and corners, with his 6ft 2in frame coming in quite useful. After nine seasons at White Hart Lane, and with his contract having expired, Sol rather spoilt his reputation with Tottenham fans by signing for their bitter rivals Arsenal. He moved to Portsmouth in 2006. In his 365 games for Spurs he scored 18 goals.

Jimmy Cantrell
Centre forward 1912-1923

	Appearances	Goals
League	159	74
FA Cup	15	10
Other	20	11
TOTAL	194	

When Derbyshire-born Cantrell com-pleted eleven years with Tottenham, he had registered 95 goals from 194 games; one goal every two matches, not a bad record for a 5ft 9in centre forward. What made this more remarkable was the fact that Cantrell was approaching thirty when he joined Spurs in 1912. He was in the cup-winning side of 1921 and was still leading the line when only a few weeks short of his thirty-ninth birthday. He was the oldest player to appear for Tottenham when he played his last game in April 1923. Jimmy was still not finished, and stepped down a pace when spending his last seasons with Sutton Town; he finally retired in 1925.

His career started with the Chesterfield Schools team and on leaving school he played for local sides Bulwell Red Rose, Bulwell White Star and Hucknall. In 1908 he signed for Notts County and in four years at Meadow Lane he was top scorer for three. Although selected as a reserve for England, he never got to play for his country. In an era when it was not illegal to charge the goalkeeper into the net still clutch-ing the ball, Cantrell was not one of the biggest built of centre forwards, relying more on skill. He was a thinking leader of the forward line and good with either foot; this suited Spurs when they signed him in October 1912. Straightaway he was put into the team, playing his first game against Manchester United, and he was soon figuring on the scoring list in his second match when he got two goals in a 3-3 draw with Aston Villa.

When the First World War broke out he assisted his former club Notts County, as he was stationed back in the Midlands, and afterwards settled back at Tottenham at the age of thirty-seven, holding on to his spot in the team where his regular scoring was welcomed. Jimmy was a fixture in the Spurs line-up when they won the Second Division championship in 1919/20, and when they became FA Cup winners in 1921. When Bert Bliss joined Spurs and struck up a fruitful partnership with Cantrell they were looked upon as the most deadly strike force in the country. But this did not stop Tottenham being relegated in 1915 just as the First World War started, and Cantrell did not appear for Spurs again until 1919. After he retired from playing the game Jimmy took up another sport, and was soon a renowned professional golfer. He passed away in 1960 at the age of seventy-eight.

Stephen Carr
Defender 1992-2004

	Appearances	Goals
League	226	7
FA Cup	17	0
League Cup	23	1
Other	57 (15)	2
TOTAL	338	

Born in Dublin in 1976, Stephen Carr joined Spurs straight from Donahies Community School as a trainee in July 1992, holding down a place in the senior youth side in his first year at White Hart Lane, and upgraded to a professional in 1993. Stephen represented the Republic of Ireland Schoolboys 13 times, the Youth side 10 times and the Under-21 squad 12 times, and is now the first name to be entered at no.2 when the Republic of Ireland team is selected. He progressed through the Spurs system to stake a regular place in the line-up and was a great favourite with all the supporters. He made his debut for Tottenham away at Burnley on 22 September 1993 in a Coca-Cola (Football League) Cup fixture, and four days later played in the Premiership at Ipswich Town. It was a long wait before he was in the League side again, as he missed out in the next season, but he made 30 appearances in 1996/97, and was in the XI from then on. In 1994 Stephen was named Young Player of the Year at Tottenham, the award being the prestigious Sidney Wale Challenge Cup. He was a regular for Spurs who loved to attack and took opponents on whenever he could; who can forget his well struck goal at a wet White Hart Lane against the mighty Manchester United? During 1999, in one of the seemingly endless tables that look into what makes football tick, Stephen was listed as an accurate distributor of the ball who succeeded with 755 of his 966 passes; a rate of seventy-five per cent. At that time Carr had made ninety-one attacking runs with the ball and sent across fifty-six crosses. Stephen made well over 300 appearances for Spurs despite missing the whole of the 2001/02 campaign with an injury that simply refused to go away. In 2003/04 he was rewarded for his efforts with a long spell as captain of the side when Jamie Redknapp suffered a long-term injury, and he revelled in the post. Carr was a model of consistency at White Hart Lane for ten years, and left for Newcastle United in 2004.

Martin Chivers

Striker 1968-1977

	Appearances	Goals
League	268 (10)	118
FA Cup	22 (2)	11
League Cup	33	23
Europe	32	22
Other	47 (1)	28
TOTAL	415	

Chivers joined his home-town club Southampton straight from school, where he had gained five O levels; further education did not appeal to him and he made football his career. He played for the Southampton Schools Under-15 side and the Saints nursery team before stepping up to the reserves where he found his extreme liking for scoring goals. Chivers signed professional forms at the start of the 1962/63 season and made his debut in a 1-0 win at Charlton Athletic. Impressive displays soon saw him make the first of a record 17 appearances for England Under-23s. In the Saints' promotion year of 1965/66, Chivers scored 30 goals in 39 matches.

Although playing in the First Division, Martin looked for a move to one of the top clubs, and Bill Nicholson convinced him that Tottenham was that club. He signed for Spurs in January 1968, Southampton receiving £125,000, a British record at that time, and Frank Saul, valued at £45,000. In his first game in a Spurs shirt, at Sheffield Wednesday, Chivers 'did a Greaves', scoring in a 2-1 victory. He followed this with two goals at Old Trafford in the FA Cup. Top goalscorers, Chivers and Greaves, played together for the best part of two years at White Hart Lane and scored 98 goals between them. This was in spite of a long layoff by Chivers with a serious knee injury, which needed surgery; he missed a huge section of one season.

Returning to action in 1969, he struggled to find his form and was in and out of the team as manager Nicholson tried many ways to get the gentle giant back to the form that saw his arrival at Tottenham. More use of his weight was a factor in his game and he was compared with bustling Bobby Smith. Gradually his confidence returned, and five goals in a reserve match at Northampton saw his career restarted. His two goals in the League Cup final victory over Aston Villa in 1971 proved once and for all that he was back in business, with more aggression and use of his 6ft frame. He had hit the back of the net 13 times in cup matches alone that year. He still looked too casual and indeed clumsy at times, but he was deceptive and extremely talented.

Another Chivers weapon came to the fore: his long throw-ins, which were as dangerous as corner kicks. Then came his selection for England, and his debut against Malta, in Valletta, in February 1971, in a team that also included

his Spurs teammates Mullery and Peters. Chivers went on to gain 24 full caps for his country, scoring 13 goals. At this time he was acknowledged as the finest all-round centre forward in the world, as supporters waited with baited breath whenever Chivers received the ball within shooting range of the opponents' goal.

Spurs had a very productive trio, as Chivers linked up with Gilzean and Peters, which produced many goals. These three were also capable of surging through on their own when passing between them was not on. But it was Martin Chivers who was the goalscorer-in-chief that people came to see, and he never let them down. Some particular instances come to mind. A thirty-five-yard free-kick in the first leg of the UEFA Cup final at Wolves in 1972, a delicate flick with the head from a Peters

free-kick against Malta, and a curling shot which beat Gordon Banks at Stoke.

After 415 appearances and 202 goals, Martin left Tottenham for Swiss club Servette in July 1976 following a poor season in which he managed 9 goals from 38 games. Chivers's last two Spurs appearances were coming on as substitute in the last two games of the season. Two years later he returned to England for a season at Norwich City, and another at Brighton & Hove Albion, before a player-manager spell at Dorchester Town. 1981 saw him in Norway as player-coach for Vard FC, plus a short spell in the same post with Barnet. He can still be seen playing in the gentle world of the Spurs Legends team, which he runs, as well as raising money for charities. He is also active as one of the hosts in a suite at White Hart Lane each home match.

Harry Clarke

Centre half 1948-1957

	Appearances	Goals
League	295	4
FA Cup	27	0
Other	58	0
TOTAL	380	

Harry Clarke arrived at Tottenham from Lovells Athletic in March 1949, and many assumed that he was Welsh. He was, however, born at Woodford Green on the outskirts of London on 23 February 1923. He played for Woodford Schools and, on leaving school, played with local youth teams. He joined the RAF in 1942 and for three years was stationed in the West Indies, where he didn't play much football. When he did, however, he managed to play alongside some professional players and this helped his football immensely. Back in England, he was a regular in his RAF station team in Wiltshire, and he then joined Lovells Athletic, a club from Wales who were in the Southern League. He spent three years with Lovells, and during his time at the club they won the Welsh League three seasons running, as well as the Welsh Senior Cup in 1947/48.

Spurs then stepped in and soon he was transferred to them in March 1949. They were so confident in him that he was pitched straight into the first team versus Luton Town at White Hart Lane on 19 March 1949, at the ripe old age of twenty-six. After that debut match, 6ft 3in Harry was an ever-present for the next two seasons, with 101 consecutive appearances. He was not a goalscorer but more of a 'stopper', in an old fashioned way, and only scored four goals while at Tottenham, these all coming in the 1955/56 season. Harry was almost unequalled in the air and, for such a tall man, was just as good with the ball at his feet; his long legs gave him an advantage over most forwards and his long strides made it look that that he was a casual player. He also built up a great understanding with goalkeeper Ted Ditchburn and both full-backs, and from the big booted clearance he had possessed when he arrived at White Hart Lane he soon developed something more constructive.

He was a steady centre half in the Spurs team, who were champions of the Second Division and First Division in successive seasons under manager Arthur Rowe (1949/50 and 1950/51). When Alf Ramsey moved to Ipswich, Harry became the Tottenham captain in 1955. He retired from playing in 1957, taking a coaching post at White Hart Lane until he went to Llanelli as manager; later he also had a spell at Romford as manager. Harry represented England 'B' in March 1954 and made his one appearance for England against Scotland the following month. He made 380 appearances for Spurs.

Tommy Clay
Full-back 1913-1929

	Appearances	Goals
League	318	23
FA Cup	33	1
Wartime	106	7
Other	49	7
TOTAL	506	

Tommy was an important member of the Tottenham Hotspur team who won the FA Cup in 1921. Born in Leicester in 1892, he played his first competitive games with Belvoir Sunday School team and joined his local side Leicester Fosse in 1911, before being swept to White Hart Lane for a 'stiff fee' two years later. As a right-back his uncanny positional skill was his best quality and he always gave an impression of coolness in his play, although he was a hard but fair tackling player when needed. He was very much admired by Spurs supporters, especially the younger element. For many years Clay was at the heart of the Tottenham defence and was the club captain when they won the championship of Division Two in 1919/20, but handed it over to Grimsdell the next season when they won the FA Cup.

During the First World War, Tommy managed to play fairly regularly for Spurs, although he was a guest for Notts County when in the Midlands. He was also the club's penalty taker at this time and his misses were few; placing, rather than hitting the ball and relying on speed. His career at White Hart Lane was one of the longest and most impressive of all players; he was with Tottenham just under fifteen years. He actually played in goal for one match, being selected in that position when both regulars Hunter and Jacques were not available. This happened on 26 March 1921 at Sunderland and he kept a clean sheet in a 1-0 Spurs victory.

Clay played in an international trial match in 1919, but did not play for his country until

March 1920, when he was selected for England against Wales at Highbury. He went on to win more caps for England. Something that forever haunted Tommy Clay happened on 4 March 1920, in the FA Cup match versus Aston Villa at White Hart Lane. Tottenham were going well in the cup rounds that year; their 3 victories had brought them 11 goals with only 1 conceded, and a tragic mis-kick by the unflappable Clay gave the Villa a single-goal win. Just two days later Tommy won his first England cap – the ultimate in the highs and lows of football.

In 1929, at the age of thirty-seven, he was not retained by Spurs and he accepted a post as player-coach at Northfleet, the nursery club for Tottenham, in June. Although he took on a public house in St Albans, he was with Northfleet until 1931 when he became a coach with St Albans City. Tommy Clay made 506 appearances for Spurs, all at right-back except the one match in goal, and scored 38 goals. He passed away in Southend in 1949.

Ralph Coates
Forward 1971-1981

	Appearances	Goals
League	173 (15)	14
FA Cup	11 (1)	0
League Cup	19 (3)	1
Europe	26	9
Other	48 (9)	6
TOTAL	305	

When Ralph joined Tottenham Hotspur from Burnley in May 1971, aged twenty-five, he was already an England international with two caps to his name. At Turf Moor he had played eight times for the England Under-23s and the Football League XI. Spurs splashed out £190,000 for his services and his first two games as a Tottenham player were for England; his third and fourth caps. Born at Hetton-Le-Hole in County Durham in 1946, he was a centre forward at school and represented Durham Schools; on leaving school he was not picked up by any League club. Coates then took a job at Eppleton Colliery and played his football with the works side. It was then that Burnley took notice and they took him on as an amateur in 1961, and then as a professional in June 1963. He established himself as a promising player and found his best position in midfield. Alf Ramsey called him up for England and he made his first appearance versus Northern Ireland in April 1970.

His Spurs debut was at Wolves in the Football League Cup in August 1971. At first, Ralph was played as an orthodox winger at White Hart Lane. It could be said that during his nine years at Tottenham he never really settled down to any position in the team, but played his best in whichever position he found himself in. There was no doubt he could win a game with a quick dash towards goal or a flick to set up a scoring chance. It was in the last League game of the 1971/72 season that Ralph earned some respect from the Spurs followers. It was against Arsenal at Highbury when he took possession of the ball inside his own half and ran past several Arsenal defenders, leaving them behind with his burst of speed, then gave the Arsenal goalkeeper no chance with an immaculate goal.

The different numbers worn on his shirt in his time at White Hart Lane, and his seemingly having been used as a fill-in player, shows that he was moved around the Tottenham side. Coates was a member of the Spurs side which won the UEFA Cup in 1972, and reached the final again in 1974. But his one moment of glory came when he scored the winning goal against Norwich City in the Football League Cup final in 1973, after coming on as a substitute. He left Spurs for the St George club in Sydney, Australia, returning to home shores and Orient on a free transfer. Later he played out his days at Hertford Heath and Ware. His 305 Spurs appearances saw him score 30 goals.

Alfie Conn
Forward 1974-1977

	Appearances	Goals
League	35 (3)	6
FA Cup	2	0
League Cup	1 (2)	1
Other	11 (5)	3
TOTAL	59	

Although spending only three years at Tottenham, in the mid-1970s, twenty-two-year-old Alfie Conn was a character in every sense of the word, and he also displayed the skills to go with it. He was Bill Nicholson's last signing, coming to White Hart Lane in June 1974 from Glasgow Rangers for a fee of £140,000. He was one of the first Spurs players to follow modern fashion with his long hair; manager Nicholson was not happy with this but he recognised the magical skills in Conn. Alfie began his football at school and was soon selected for Scotland Schools. As a schoolboy, he had played rugby for East of Scotland before deciding soccer was his first choice, joining Scottish junior club Edina and then Musselburgh. In October 1968 he was transferred to Rangers where he made his debut in their first team when only sixteen, and he was a member of the winning sides in the 1971 Scottish League Cup, the 1973 Scottish Cup, and the European Cup-Winners' Cup in 1972.

At White Hart Lane he had made just one appearance as a substitute in the Football League Cup versus Middlesborough, before Terry Neil took over as manager. Alfie Conn was a crowd entertainer, which the Spurs fans delighted in,

and he became a cult figure; but he frustrated managers and coaches alike. His first League match for Tottenham was against Newcastle United at St James Park, and he celebrated with a hat-trick in a Spurs win of 5-2. He had come into the team when Chivers was injured, and played the remaining matches of that season at outside right. A series of injuries, mainly through his type of play, led to him being out of the Spurs side on numerous occasions.

Two sides of Conn's thinking were seen in the match against Leeds in April 1975, as he tricked his path past three defenders to score a great goal, and then sat on the ball during the playing of the game. He form was so good that he was capped twice by Scotland in 1975, and played three games for the Scotland Under-23 XI; but after this he was in and out of the side and spent much of the time in Spurs' reserves.

He joined Celtic in 1977 where he enjoyed success in their cup-winning sides and the Scottish League title. Then followed spells in the USA for three different clubs before returning to Britain to sign for Hearts, Blackpool and Motherwell and taking on the post of manager at Coatbridge. His 59 appearances at Tottenham saw him score 10 goals.

Jabez Darnell

Half-back 1905-1919

	Appearances	Goals
S. League	34	1
W. League	21	0
FA Cup	11	0
League	153	3
Other	108	1
TOTAL	327	

When Jabez Darnell signed the form binding him to Tottenham Hotspur it was not known that he would take this so literally, as he was to be at White Hart Lane for the greater part of his life. He played until he was thirty-six years of age, his last match being a 2-2 draw with Millwall in the London Combination on 18 April 1919. This game was played on the Homerton ground, which was Clapton Orient's home ground, as White Hart Lane had been commandeered in 1915 by the Ministry of Munitions and made into a gas mask factory. Buildings were erected on the terraces and under the stands, and 11 million gas masks were made during the First World War. At the end of the war, Darnell retired.

Born in Potton, in Bedfordshire, he had started his football career with Northampton Town and was signed by Spurs in 1905, making his debut almost immediately in a 1-1 draw with Queens Park Rangers, away, on 11 September 1905.

This match was played before Tottenham were a Football League club, when they were in the Western League; the Spurs were then playing in two different leagues with the Southern League being the main one. Jabez flitted equally between the two competitions, playing at wing half. He was noted as a tough-tackling defender who would stop at nothing for the cause of Tottenham Hotspur, and it was nearly three seasons before he scored his first goal for the club.

Darnell was a link between the Spurs FA Cup winning sides of 1901 and 1921; he played with Morris, Hughes and Sandy Tait from the 1901 side and some of his fellow team members in 1919 were Grimsdell, Clay, Walden and Cantrell, who carried off the FA Cup in 1921. He played as often as he could throughout the war, mostly in his proper position but often filling in on the wing or at centre half. When Spurs were elected into the Football League, Darnell was in the side for the first match, against FA Cup holders Wolverhampton Wanderers, on 1 September 1908, which Tottenham won 3-0, on a blustery and cloudy Thursday afternoon in front of an estimated 20,000 crowd.

After Darnell finished playing he was still loyal to his only club and took on the post of assistant trainer right up to 1946, when he retired at the age of sixty-two, making it just over forty years of service to Tottenham Hotspur. He made 327 appearances and scored 5 goals in his career, a true dedication to his only club.

	Appearances	Goals
League	400	100
FA Cup	38	12
Other	53	26
TOTAL	491	

Another player who served Tottenham for thirteen years, Jimmy was a local lad, born in Edmonton in December 1900, and was a firm favourite with the supporters of the Spurs. He firmly cemented his place in Tottenham folklore with the winning goal in the 1921 FA Cup final, as rain lashed Stamford Bridge. He was the youngest player on the field that day, and this was only his second season at the club. After leaving Montague School, Jimmy played with local junior clubs Park Avenue and Gothic Works before Tottenham spotted him playing for Edmonton Ramblers and brought him to White Hart Lane as an amateur when he was just sixteen.

During the First World War, Spurs allowed him to play for Clapton Orient and fine-tune his skills. Even then, he had his band of supporters who only came to watch Orient because he was included. The war came to an end and Dimmock, being an amateur, could be signed by any club. Although Arsenal and the Orient wanted him on their books, Jimmy decided his place was at White Hart Lane, much to Spurs' delight. He turned professional in May 1919 and soon forced his way into the Spurs' League side; his first match was away to Lincoln City on 4 October 1919. Seven weeks passed before he was called into the senior side again, at home versus Nottingham Forest. Dimmock grabbed one of the Tottenham goals in a 5-2 win, and kept his position this time, for the rest of that season, adding five more goals to his name. Spurs had one of their best seasons ever to finish top of the Second Division and gain promotion to the First Division; suffering only four League defeats in doing so.

Long-standing Spurs supporters held the view that Dimmock was the best winger ever seen at the club. He was certainly a brilliant outside left and went from success to success, becoming a firm favourite. When he went off on one of his famous dribbles along Tottenham's left wing it seemed he was playing for himself at times, but manager Peter McWilliam – and later Billy Minter and Percy Smith – was happy at his displays throughout the twenties. Jimmy possessed a hard shot in both of his feet, and it looked as if he was heading for a long international career when he was selected in two England trial matches in February 1921. Although he had a rare talent this was not rewarded with a cap for England until a year later, in the game against

A fine illustration of Jimmy Dimmock, which could be used for coaching purposes. Right foot alongside the ball and eyes fully focused. He was one of the first Spurs players to wear his shirt outside his shorts.

Scotland at Hampden Park on 9 April 1921. England also had Bert Smith, Arthur Grimsdell and Bert Bliss from Tottenham Hotspur in the team. Continuing to sparkle for Spurs, he was not picked for England again until 1926, when they lost to Wales, and just one more cap followed.

When Tottenham were struggling to fill the centre forward place in the team, in the 1922/23 season, Jimmy Dimmock was even tried out in this position; but this didn't solve the problem and he was quickly reinstated at no.11. He was not really a goalscorer, although he weighed in with some important strikes in his career. These included both goals at Highbury against north London arch rivals Arsenal on 30 September 1922, and his only hat-trick in the FA Cup in the 5-0 victory over West Ham United in January 1926. Late in his playing days, Jimmy became the penalty king for Spurs, with misses occurring rarely, but he began to put on some extra weight and got a bit slower.

In 1932 Tottenham allowed him to move to the Thames club, who folded at the end of the season, and he moved to Clapton Orient before finally moving to Ashford in the Kent League, where he retired after a few months. His popularity with Spurs fans never waned and, when in the Second World War he was invited to take part in a Red Cross charity match, two coaches took them to cheer on their old hero. He passed away just before Christmas 1972. His 491 appearances brought him 138 goals.

Ted Ditchburn
Goalkeeper 1939-1959

	Appearances	Goals
League	419	0
FA Cup	34	0
Wartime	54	0
Other	68	0
TOTAL	575	

One of the best goalkeepers to ever wear the jersey of Tottenham Hotspur, Ditchburn was with the club for twenty years, the supporters all heaving a sigh of relief when they saw the big frame of Ted running onto the field for the start of a game. He had a spell from April 1946 to March 1954 when he missed just two League and cup games, and set up a record of 247 consecutive appearances. But for the interruption of the Second World War, he would certainly have made many more. Ted was born at Gillingham, in Kent, on 24 October 1921, the son of a boxer, the profession towards which he was leaning before settling for a football career. He represented Kent Schools and had a trial for England Schools before joining Northfleet Paper Mills, from where he joined Spurs' ground staff in 1937. In June of the next year he signed amateur forms for the club and found himself in Kent again with Northfleet.

Tottenham upgraded him to professional in May 1939 but, before things got underway, the war intervened, although he impressed in the Spurs Public Trial match in August 1939, putting on a promising display. When all players in the country were advised to return home, Ditchburn started to play for Dartford. It was not long before he was called up to the RAF and his postings put him quite a way from London, playing in only the last two matches in the first war season. Missing all the next season, when he was playing for Aberdeen, he did manage to help Spurs in a reasonable number of matches during the war. He was selected many times during the war for RAF teams, Combined Services, and twice for an unofficial England side versus Wales and Scotland.

At the end of the transitional season of 1945/46, Ditchburn was quickly demobbed and went straight into the Spurs team. League Champions Birmingham City regarded him so highly they borrowed him for their last game. From then on Ted Ditchburn was a regular

'Never just stop the ball if you can possibly catch it.' Ditchburn gathers the ball in safely in the FA Cup tie against Arsenal at Highbury.

between the posts at Tottenham and was an ever-present in the Spurs team that won Division Two and Division One in 1950 and 1951. For one so tall, 6ft 1in, he was remarkably agile as he flung himself across the goal and bravely at the forwards' feet, and at a time when it was allowed to touch the goalkeeper, not many opponents ventured to challenge the Tottenham custodian. He had, however, a very weak kick and found he could throw the ball further and more accurately. Many Spurs moves started from a throw out to Alf Ramsey at right-back, with whom he had built up an almost telepathic understanding.

Ted Ditchburn was the height of consistency for many years and was picked as a reserve for the England matches on numerous occasions. It was unfortunate that he was at his best when other great goalkeepers were about, such as Frank Swift and Gil Merrick. Ted had to wait a while before being given his chance to keep goal for England, although he appeared regularly for the Football League, and was in the England World Cup party in 1950. Ted finally broke into the England team, earning his first full cap in December 1948, but he was not a regular and only played five more times in the next eight years. He was the model of consistency year after year, and was one of the most important figures in Arthur Rowe's 'push and run' team of the early fifties. Ditchburn was a goalkeeper who was always in charge whenever the ball came into the Spurs penalty area, and he reminded everyone, with a loud shout, as to what he was going to do or what he expected from his teammates.

As the 1950s progressed Ted sometimes lost out to younger goalkeeper Ron Reynolds, but looked upon that as a challenge and won his place back. A broken finger at Chelsea in August virtually ended his top-flight career, and he joined Romford in 1959, becoming their player-manager, before retiring in 1965. His appearances for Spurs totalled 575.

	Appearances	Goals
League	101 (2)	53
FA Cup	7	2
League Cup	10	7
Other	21 (4)	13
TOTAL	145	

Born in Dundee in 1949, Duncan was the first buy of Spurs' new manager Terry Neil in October 1974. A Scottish schoolboy trialist, he turned professional with Dundee straight from school, and was loaned as a junior, at first to Broughty Thistle, but soon found his way into the Dundee line-up. Duncan was the top scorer for Dundee when £150,000 brought him to White Hart Lane.

John never quite made it into the Scotland team, coming close when he was a substitute on two occasions without getting onto the pitch; he did, however, play for the Scottish League versus the Football League, scoring both goals in a 2-2 draw. Tottenham had begun the season in a poor way, and out of the opening 12 games they had won only 3. They occupied a lowly place in the league, and had also changed managers. With Chivers still at the club, the arrival of Duncan was hopefully to form a scoring partnership. Duncan was handed the no.11 shirt and placed straight into the First XI at Luton Town on 26 October 1974. He opened his account in the following match with both Spurs goals in a 2-2 draw.

Duncan was an awkward goalscorer at times, meaning many of his goals came from knee or thigh as opposed to the conventional way, but all goals counted as long as they ended in the back of the net. He arrived at Tottenham to help ward off the spectre of relegation, and to a degree he succeeded, but only just. He ended up as Spurs top scorer with 12 goals, and the following season he topped the list with 25; he was averaging a goal every other game. He was then sidelined for several long periods with a back injury, which limited his appearances in the 1976/77 season, and Tottenham missed his tally of goals as they dropped into Division Two. Duncan top-scored with 20 goals as Tottenham bounded back into the First Division at the first attempt.

He played his last game for Spurs in the 7-0 defeat at Anfield. He moved to Derby County, then joined Scunthorpe, taking over as manager. He held this post with Hartlepool before taking Chesterfield to the Fourth Division championship. Three years at Ipswich Town followed and then a return to Chesterfield for more success. Duncan's record at Spurs was 75 goals from 145 appearances.

Len Duquemin
Centre forward 1945-1957

	Appearances	Goals
League	275	114
FA Cup	33	17
Wartime	1	0
Other	65	53
TOTAL	374	

The 'Duke', as he was known, was a real legend at White Hart Lane. He came to Spurs from Guernsey in the Channel Islands, where he had kept a low profile when they were occupied during the Second World War. Len started with Guernsey Schools and was with a club named Vauxbelet when he was recommended to Spurs. He arrived in north London as a twenty-one-year-old and, after signing amateur forms, was given a trial. He was loaned out to Chelmsford City where Arthur Rowe was manager. Rowe advised Tottenham of Len's ability and he was subsequently placed in the Spurs reserves, his first match coming against Marlow in February 1946. After five games, he was given an outing for the first team at Fulham on 9 March 1946; still as an amateur.

Strangely, Len did not play in any First XI matches the next season, but was at centre forward at the beginning of the 1947/48 season, and started to show he was a prolific goalscorer. He was the top marksman in this season with 24, which included 8 in the FA Cup, where he got a goal in each round as Spurs reached the semi-final. He was a workhorse type of player who led his forward line with dedication for close on thirteen years, especially in the glory teams of the late forties and early fifties.

Some folk thought Len would find it much harder to score goals in the First Division, but he proved them all wrong as his scoring rate only eased up slightly. Others were asking why a player of Duquemin's quality was not playing for England, so high was he held in esteem. Len did not have the high skills of others, but was always relied upon to give his best for his club every week. Tottenham reached the FA Cup semi-finals again in 1953, only to lose to Blackpool once more, the 'Duke' getting Tottenham's lone goal. Spurs seemed to lose heart after yet another semi-final loss, and it was Duquemin who kept plugging away, with 24 goals as the top scorer once again, to keep the Spurs quite high in tenth place.

Everyone who played in the same team as Len described him as a players' player who was always on hand to hold up the ball and create the opening for his teammates. As well as notching important goals, his heading ability was an important factor in his play. After seeing off the challenges of younger centre forwards at Tottenham, Duquemin finally left White Hart Lane for Bedford Town, and after spells at Hastings and Romford, he retired from the game. In 374 appearances for Spurs he scored 184 goals.

Terry Dyson
Winger 1954-1965

	Appearances	Goals
League	184	41
FA Cup	16	6
Europe	9	8
Other	30 (5)	13
TOTAL	244	

Terry was a pint-sized winger who more than held his place in the star-studded Tottenham Hotspur double winning team of 1961, in which he only missed two matches. He showed he could also score goals, ending the glory season with 17 to his credit including one in the FA Cup final against Leicester City. Terry was the son of a jockey, 'Ginger' Dyson, so it was not surprising he stood at just over 5ft and weighed about ten stone, but this never deterred him in his quest for the best at White Hart Lane. Born in Malton in Yorkshire on 29 November 1934, he first played for Scarborough as a teenager before signing as an amateur for Tottenham in 1955, doing his National Service at the time. When discharged from the army four months later, he was upgraded to professional status. With George Robb and Terry Medwin installed on the wing at Tottenham, Terry had to wait for his chance, as he was mostly the understudy when they were not available. He loved every minute of his football and it showed in his frantic celebrations when he scored a goal He was a hyperactive footballer who hardly ever stopped for breath.

Terry made his Tottenham debut on 19 March 1955 in a Football League game versus Sheffield United which Spurs won 5-0. This was Terry's only appearance of the season and he increased his matches by three more games the next year. He opened his scoring account in his sixth appearance, and at the beginning of the 1960/61 season Terry still had only 25 games under his belt. This all changed in the 'double' season when Dyson was pencilled in for the no.11 berth, with Cliff Jones playing on the other flank. Terry only missed two matches in that season and had 17 goals to his credit. In Europe he was not the sort of player the other teams had met, and he carried on playing and scoring as only he knew how; his crowning moment was two goals in the European Cup Winners Cup final in a 5-1 win over Atletico Madrid.

After eleven years at White Hart Lane he crossed London to Fulham for £5,000. Three seasons were spent at Craven Cottage before he joined Colchester United, and then a spell in non-League football and retirement beckoned. His 244 Tottenham appearances got him 68 goals.

Justin Edinburgh
Full-back 1990-2000

	Appearances	Goals
League	190 (23)	1
FA Cup	27 (1)	0
League Cup	28 (4)	0
Europe	4 (2)	0
Other	39 (15)	1
TOTAL	333	

Born in Basildon on 18 December 1969, Justin began his football career when he was taken on by Southend United under the YTS scheme in the summer of 1986, and he flourished so well he was upgraded to professional status just two years later. His debut for Southend came on 25 November 1887, against Brighton & Hove Albion, in the Associated Members Cup, and this was his only game of the season. When he was selected the next season, he took his opportunity well and made 47 appearances in the next two seasons.

Spotted by Tottenham, he was taken on for a loan period of three months from January to March 1990, but he was not given a try out for the senior XI. He returned to Southend and helped them gain promotion to the Third Division. Justin had impressed enough at Tottenham and he transferred to Spurs in July 1990 for £150,000. The raw edges were beginning to be smoothed over as he made the breakthrough when there were several injuries

at the club. It was 26 September 1990 that saw him play his first game for Spurs at Hartlepool United in the Football League Cup, although he had played in a pre-season friendly for Tottenham at Shelbourne the previous month.

His quickness in the tackle, some said too impetuous at times, and an eager will to succeed and keep his place stood out as he chalked up 21 appearances in his first season at White Hart Lane. He had been acquired by Tottenham as a replacement for Pat van den Hauwe in the long run, and had benefited when the left-back was injured; Justin played all the pre-season friendlies before the 1990/91 campaign. When the League started in earnest, Edinburgh was back in the reserve team and his elevation to the First XI saw him playing at right-back – but he soon laid claim to the other flank. He wound up his first season with one of his best performances in the FA Cup semi-final against Arsenal, then winning his first cup medal when Spurs beat Nottingham Forest at Wembley; not bad for a newcomer.

Edinburgh suffered a dip in form for a while but fought through this lean patch to raise his game. By the closing matches of the 1992/93 season he had learned to defend with more poise, and his attacking forays down the left wing carved out chances for the Spurs strikers. When he left Spurs for Portsmouth he had made 333 appearances and scored twice.

John Elkes
Inside forward, centre half 1923-1929

	Appearances	Goals
League	191	50
FA Cup	10	1
Other	12	6
TOTAL	213	

Albert John Elkes, known better by all as Jack, was at Tottenham for most of the 1920s, mainly in the inside forward berth, but he was equally at ease playing at centre half. Elkes was born in Snedshill, in Shropshire, on the last day of the year 1894, and started his career at amateur clubs Wellington and Wellington St Georges before entering the professional ranks with Stalybridge Celtic and Shifnal Town. Then Birmingham City introduced him to Football League action, and he spent four years at St Andrews before Southampton took him to the South Coast. A two-goal debut for the Saints was followed by a collarbone injury, but Spurs had seen enough and they brought him to White Hart Lane in May 1923 for a fee of £1,000.

His first Tottenham match was at home against Middlesbrough, and he played his first season mostly at inside left, with four games at inside right and one at centre forward. Centre half was a problem position for Spurs and Elkes found himself in the no.5 shirt for the opening games of the next season. It was in the forward line that he really excelled and he linked up with Jimmy Dimmock to form a more than useful left-wing pair. For some reason, Elkes spent the whole 1926/27 season at centre half for Spurs, which his 6ft frame helped greatly.

For such a tall player, Jack Elkes was good to have on your side due to his dribbling skills and his temperament; he refused to accept defeat. He was also unlucky to be at Tottenham when they were having some barren years in the bottom half of the First Division, before dropping into the Second Division in 1928. He played for the Football League four times and in four international trial matches, but did not win an England cap; he came nearest being named as a reserve for one England match. He was a member of the FA party that toured Australia in 1925, and in the same year was selected for the Professionals versus Amateurs in the FA Charity Shield. He was best known as an attacker and his 57 goals for Tottenham came in 213 appearances.

Elkes was not retained at White Hart Lane in April 1929, so he joined Middlesbrough and then moved on to Watford in 1933, where he played just one season before leaving the professional scene. Stafford Rangers and Oakengates Town were his non-League clubs when he retired and turned to coaching in 1937. He ended his coaching career at the Ford Motor Works Football Club.

	Appearances	Goals
League	300	14
FA Cup	32	2
League Cup	30	0
Europe	35	3
Other	37	1
TOTAL	434	

For nine years Mike England was at the heart of the Tottenham defence. He had stepped straight into the team at the start of the 1966/67 season, and in his first campaign at White Hart Lane he only missed one match, that being the Football League Cup defeat at West Ham, which was the first time Spurs had entered that particular competition. Tottenham finished the season with an unbeaten run in the First Division, from 14 January to 13 May, conceding only ten goals, and a grand finale at Wembley, winning the FA Cup in a game against Chelsea. In their cup run they had a goal record of 16 for, 3 against.

The influence of Mike England was uppermost in this success and he rarely missed a match, except when he was injured. Regarded as the best centre half in Britain, he had joined Blackburn Rovers as an apprentice in 1957 straight from his school, Tsgol Dinas Basing in North Wales, having been born at nearby Greenfield on 2 December 1941. He was a member of Blackburn Rovers' successful Youth Cup-winning team of 1959. As a sixteen-year-old he had also represented Holywell Schools and Flint Schools. At the outset, he played at outside right, half-back and centre forward at Blackburn. He then found his true position, centre half, which enabled him to use his height of 6ft 2in to the best advantage.

Spurs had paid £95,000, a record at that time for a defender, for England's transfer, snatching him from under the noses of Manchester United. Mike was a key part in the rebuilding of Tottenham as the double-winning team began to break up. An added bonus was his strength in the air, which was a great help when he moved into the opposing penalty area for corners and free-kicks. He was often moved upfield during a match to force a goal, but in a mid-season experiment in November 1968, when Chivers suffered a bad injury and goals were hard to come by, he was selected at centre forward. Although he did grab 2 goals in 5 games, he was soon back in his best position. Tottenham won the Football League Cup in 1971, but England had to sit this one out with an injured ankle. He did, however, play in the UEFA Cup-winning side in 1972 and the successful 1973 Football League Cup side. He was capped for Wales 44 times, captaining them also. At only thirty-three he decided to retire, in 1975, with ankle problems. He had one last season with Cardiff City, and short spells in America before he became manager of Wales for just over seven seasons. He was awarded the MBE in 1984.

	Appearances	Goals
League	133 (4)	2
FA Cup	7	0
League Cup	13	0
Europe	22 (3)	2
Other	20 (2)	1
TOTAL	204	

Ray was born just up the road from White Hart Lane at Edmonton on 20 September 1949. Standing out in his schooldays, he soon found himself selected for Edmonton Schoolboys, then the Middlesex Schools team. Possessing a great turn of speed, he was the first of the now recognised overlapping full-backs. Evans could also plant a good cross where it would do the most damage, and varied this with an accurate shot himself. In defence, his tackles were always well timed and strong.

Tottenham signed him as an apprentice in July 1965 and upgraded him to full professional status in May 1967, by which time he was already an England Youth international. With Kinnear and Beal fighting over the right-back position, Evans had to take a back seat in his early days at White Hart Lane, but made his debut on 24 March 1969. He couldn't have picked a more difficult baptism than a north London clash versus Arsenal at Highbury. Although Spurs lost by the only goal, Ray kept his place before Beal returned and then dropped down to substitute.

For the next few seasons he was understudy to Kinnear, and had a short spell as no.6. That was until the 1971/72 season when he had a longer run in the side, sharing the position with Joe Kinnear. After missing out in the UEFA Cup final against Wolves in 1972, Ray had his best year in 1973/74, when he only missed two matches. However, he again missed out in the Football League Cup final versus Norwich City in 1973 after playing in many of the previous rounds. Despite his attacking play, it was not until 8 December 1973 that he scored his first goal for Spurs, against Stoke City at White Hart Lane, and his only other strike came later in the same season against Chelsea. He did, however, notch an important goal in Europe; the only one in the match against Vitoria Setubal.

Following seven years at Tottenham, and still not a regular, Ray moved to Millwall in January 1975 for £35,000, spending two years at the Den before another move to Fulham. He then went to America, where he spent time with St Louis Stars and California Surf, before returning to home soil and Stoke City where he finished his career; except for another two visits to America in 1983. He finished in the Indoor League in the USA and coaching the youngsters of the New World.

	Appearances	Goals
League	178	78
FA Cup	17	8
Other	8	10
TOTAL	203	

Tottenham Hotspur nearly always pick out the best in Welsh footballers, and Willie Evans was no exception. Born in Waunllwyd near Ebbw Vale on 7 October 1912, he was playing for Ebbw Vale Schools when barely old enough; his position in those days was as an inside forward, and his small frame of 5ft 6in did not deter him from taking on defenders with a swerving dribble. Willie thought that no club was interested in him, so he had joined the miners down the coal pits, and was surprised to receive an invitation from Tottenham to go to London and join their ground staff, also playing for Spurs Juniors, though they changed his position to outside left.

The idea was to nurse him along and introduce him to the football scene, but his rate of progress was very rapid as he was a born footballer, with one of the hardest shots at that time. He was loaned to Barnet and then Hayward Sports, one of Spurs' nursery clubs for the younger players on the Tottenham books. While at Hayward he was selected for the Spartan League, Middlesex and the London FA, but when the Southern Counties played him against the Northern Counties in what was seen as an amateur trial, they were disappointed to learn he was in fact Welsh and was therefore not available to play for England Amateurs.

Tottenham then signed him as a professional in 1931; he made his first appearance in the League match against Swansea Town at White Hart Lane on 7 November 1931, his nineteenth birthday, and celebrated by scoring two goals in a 6-2 win. Willie had in fact played for the first team in the final of the London FA Charity Cup against Arsenal at the end of the previous season. He was soon a regular in the Spurs side, missing only a few games during his footballing life. He also scored many goals and provided openings for others in the Spurs forward line of the early thirties, including Hunt, O'Callaghan and W. Hall.

His international career for Wales started in December 1932 against Northern Ireland, but when he had gained only six caps he suffered a serious knee injury on 7 November 1936 at Aston Villa; his career was virtually finished. He had damaged the knee earlier playing for Wales. Two operations later the injury did not improve and he was released. Fulham signed him and gambled on his recovery but Willie officially retired in 1938 without playing a game for Fulham. His 203 appearances for Spurs gave him 96 goals.

Mark Falco
Striker 1977-1987

	Appearances	Goals
League	162 (12)	68
FA Cup	15	5
League Cup	19 (3)	3
Europe	21 (4)	14
Other	76 (23)	63
TOTAL	335	

Born in Hackney on 22 October 1960, Falco had all the skills needed to be a successful striker. He had attended South Hackney School and was in turn selected for the London, Middlesex and Inner London Boys teams before signing as a Spurs apprentice in July 1977. He was upgraded to the professional ranks a year later. Mark made 5 appearances for the England Youth side in 1978/79, scoring 5 goals, before he celebrated his debut on 8 May 1979 at Bolton Wanderers with a goal in the 3-1 win.

This was Spurs first season back in the First Division after a short sojourn in the Second Division, during which they had tried six players in the no.9 shirt. But he did not really hold down a regular place in the Spurs line-up until nearly four years later, as he lingered on the edge of the Spurs squad for much of the time. He played only eight times the next season, when an injury kept him out for a while, and then only three League matches in 1980/81, again at the back end of the season.

His two goals at Wembley against Aston Villa in the Charity Shield seemed to signal his arrival and for the next 8 games he was showing his real ability, notching 6 goals, before picking up another serious injury. He had his best seasons between 1983 and 1986 when he was virtually an ever-present in the side and scored regularly, including a hat-trick away at Leicester City in April 1986. He was also the club's top scorer in

this time, registering over 20 goals each season. Falco was the modern idea of the old-type leader of the forward line; like Bobby Smith, his strong surges created many chances for him and also opened the way for his fellow players. He had been at Second Division Chelsea for a loan period in 1983 and made three appearances. His patience was rewarded when he became a member of the Tottenham side who took the UEFA Cup in 1984.

When new manager David Pleat arrived at White Hart Lane, Falco was again on the fringe and in October 1986 he joined Watford for £35,000. He stayed only briefly before transferring to Glasgow Rangers, where once again he had a short period, and he returned to England and Queens Park Rangers in December 1987. Three years later he moved to Millwall, where another injury led to his retirement in 1992. He then had a spell as player-manager at Worthing. He scored 153 goals in his 335 appearances for Spurs.

Tony Galvin
Midfield 1978-1988

	Appearances	Goals
League	194 (7)	20
FA Cup	23 (1)	2
League Cup	20 (3)	3
Europe	25	6
Other	88 (14)	16
TOTAL	375	

Tony was never given the acknowledgement he deserved for his part in the success of the Tottenham side in the eighties. Wearing the no.9 shirt but playing out wide, only a few clubs recognised his part in the team's success and his skill in the pinpointed crosses into the attacking zone. Born in Huddersfield on 12 July 1956, Galvin had been selected for Yorkshire Schools and then England Schools, but he decided to forget a career in football for a while. He concentrated on taking a Bachelor of Arts degree in Russian at Hull University, playing at times for the university team. He went on to teacher training college. Then Goole Town spotted him, and he was soon a regular in their side, which was where Spurs took notice and he joined them in January 1978 for a fee of £30,000.

He first appeared for the Spurs senior side when coming on as a substitute in a friendly against Saudi Arabia in Jeddah on 9 October 1979. He made his League debut at right wing versus Manchester City on 3 February 1978, when the Spurs manager made wholesale changes after failing to win in six matches. But Galvin was not called upon again until three substitute appearances in the middle of the next season; then from January he kept his place and helped Tottenham win the FA Cup in 1981, and again in 1982. Liverpool knew Galvin helped Spurs tick, and in the 1982 Football League Cup final he was watched closely, a marked man, and was soon taken out of the game by their close marking. It was in both legs of the UEFA Cup final that he really stood out in the win over Anderlecht.

In his time at White Hart Lane numbers meant nothing on the shirts as team formations were changing, Tony being given nearly every number in the team. He played his last game for Spurs at Nottingham Forest in May 1987, at no.7, the shirt in which he first played for Spurs. His family ties saw Tony play for the Republic of Ireland, where he won 20 caps while at Spurs. After ten years at White Hart Lane he went to Sheffield Wednesday for two seasons, and later was assistant manager to manager Ardiles at Swindon Town and Newcastle United, ending his career with a few games for Gateshead and non-League Royston. His 375 appearances for Tottenham brought him 47 goals.

Paul Gascoigne
Midfield 1988-1991

	Appearances	Goals
League	91 (1)	19
FA Cup	6	6
League Cup	13 (1)	8
Other	28 (3)	13
TOTAL	143	

Probably one of the most gifted players ever to grace White Hart Lane, it was Tottenham who possibly saw the best of Gascoigne during his all-too-short spell in north London. He was born in Gateshead on 27 May 1967 and was the local lad who made good. After playing for Gateshead and then Durham Schools he joined Newcastle as an associated schoolboy. He proceeded to rise quickly through the ranks and made his League debut for them a month before being signed as a professional.

Terry Venables brought Paul to Tottenham for £2 million in July 1988, in what was thought a gamble on a young, exuberant player, but he had already played 13 games for the England Under-21s. It was certainly fate when his first game for Spurs was away at Newcastle on 3 September 1988. He soon found that Tottenham supporters always liked someone with high skills and he settled down in the Spurs line-up with some ease – so much so that the Professional Footballers' Association in 1988 voted him Young Player of the Year. He played the game with a smile on his face – well, most times anyway – and was a richly talented player who won his way into the full England side against Denmark as a substitute, only eleven days after making his Spurs debut. Gascoigne was convinced by Tottenham that his skills could bring goals to his teammates, although a thrilling run at the opponents' defence would often do the same thing for him.

He certainly came of age at White Hart Lane and was a character who drew in the crowds all over the football world; Bobby Robson was urged to give him a regular spot in the England team. Paul was in the World Cup party of 1990 and he excelled himself once he was selected for the team. Although England did not gain any success, Gascoigne certainly did, and by his smiles and tears he came home a hero. Spurs won the FA Cup in 1991 mainly through the efforts of 'Gazza' but he rather spoilt the big occasion for himself early in the Wembley game.

He moved his talents to Lazio in Italy for £5.5 million after 46 goals for Spurs in 143 appearances. He returned to Scotland for a spell at Rangers but rather lost his way as his private life suffered. He then played at Middlesbrough and Everton, and drifted to the Far East for a spell without finding his football happiness again. In 2004 he signed for lower League Boston United as player-coach, then had an ultra-short spell as Kettering manager.

A.H. 'Jack' Gibbons

Centre forward 1937-1938, 1940-1946

	Appearances	Goals
League	27	13
FA Cup	6	5
Wartime	113	90
Other	2	1
TOTAL	148	

Most of Gibbons' football was in the Second World War with Tottenham Hotspur, when he was looked upon as one of the best amateur footballers of the 1940s. Gibbons remained an amateur player all through his football life. It was in fact his second spell with Spurs, having signed as an amateur in 1937/38; scoring at a phenomenal rate starting with his debut at Sheffield Wednesday on 16 September 1937. Born at Fulham in south-west London on 10 April 1914, he first turned out with local clubs Hayes, Uxbridge and Kingstonian before he joined Tottenham.

He linked up with Morrison at White Hart Lane to form a strong spearhead, scoring 18 goals from the 33 games he played. With two proven scorers, Spurs missed promotion by a cat's whisker, ending in fifth place in the Second Division. Jack also won his first England Amateur cap in January 1938, going on to gain seven altogether, and during the war he also represented England at senior level against Wales in 1942. His fellow players in that game included Lawton, Matthews, Mercer and Hapgood. Spurs were looking for a repeat performance the next season but Gibbons decided to throw in his lot with Brentford instead, where he played only 12 matches.

It was in the early days of season 1940/41 that he returned to Tottenham, as a flight sergeant in the RAF, which he had made his career in the 1930s. In 25 games for Spurs that season, Gibbons collected no less than 24 goals. He topped the Spurs scoring list for three seasons during the war years, but for the 1943/44 campaign he missed a complete season when he was posted abroad, spending quite a lot of time in North America. Gibbons was in much demand and represented the RAF and the FA at various times.

When not wearing the Tottenham shirt, he was always found a place in some other club's team, and these clubs included Brentford, Reading, Chelsea, Fulham and Bradford PA. Jack was Tottenham's top scorer during the war with 89 efforts, and set a record that will never be beaten, with four hat-tricks in successive games, all against Clapton Orient. After one spell at Bradford, he came back south and joined Brentford, going on to be their manager at one time, resigning in 1952. His Spurs appearances numbered 148, with 109 goals.

Alan Gilzean
Forward 1964-1975

	Appearances	Goals
League	335 (8)	93
FA Cup	40	21
League Cup	27 (1)	6
Europe	27 (1)	13
Other	62 (5)	40
TOTAL	506	

In eleven years at White Hart Lane Gilzean became a cult figure and was renowned for the subtle flicks of his head to make openings for teammates, or for placing his goals with ease to leave the goalkeeper stranded. Alan was born in Coupar Angus in Perthshire on 23 October 1938 and played his early football with his home-town juniors until he was spotted by Dundee, who signed him on amateur forms in January 1956, and eight months later upgraded him to a professional. While he was doing his National Service, Alan was loaned out by Dundee to Aldershot.

When Tottenham played a Scotland XI at White Hart Lane in the memorial match for John White, Gilzean was in the Scotland team, scoring twice and impressing manager Bill Nicholson so much he brought him to Tottenham in December 1964 for a fee of £72,500 – money well spent. He was straighta-way put into the First XI, as Nicholson had seen the skill in his new player. Alan scored over 100 goals for Dundee, and helped them win the Scottish League title in 1962, and reach the semi-final of the European Cup. His first Scotland cap against Norway quickly followed Scotland Under-23 selection in December 1963.

At Spurs he soon developed a formidable partnership with Greaves, and they were known as the 'G' men. Even when his sparse hair had developed a grey tinge, Gilzean was still accepted as one of the cleverest of strikers, with a thunderous shot when the occasion demanded. When Greaves left, Gilzean soon adapted his style to blend with Martin Chivers, who arrived from Southampton. With Tottenham, 'Gilly' gained winners' medals in the FA Cup of 1967, two Football League Cups in 1971 and 1973, and the 1972 UEFA Cup, as well as 22 caps for Scotland.

He shut the door on his eleven years at White Hart Lane on the club's tour to Mauritius, grabbing two final goals in the 5-0 win. He was chaired off the pitch at the end, showing just how much the players at Spurs thought of him. He coached for a spell in South Africa, returning to play, and score, in his testimonial at White Hart Lane versus Red Star Belgrade. A short time as manager at Stevenage was his swansong in football, after 173 goals in 506 games for Spurs.

Jimmy Greaves
Striker 1961-1970

	Appearances	Goals
League	322	220
FA Cup	36	32
League Cup	8	5
Europe	14	9
Other	40	40
TOTAL	420	

King of the goalscorers, Greaves created records wherever he went. He was born in February 1940, his father was a tube train driver and his brother and sister both became teachers, but as Jimmy said, he was football daft. During his schooldays Chelsea whisked him away to Stamford Bridge, although he was a confessed Spurs supporter. He was a star right from the start and notched up well over 100 goals for the Chelsea Juniors, and they quickly signed Jimmy up as a professional in 1957. He was in the Chelsea First XI for the opening game of the 1957/58 season against Spurs at White Hart Lane, where he was to shine in the future. After only six games he was selected for England Under-23s and scored twice against Bulgaria at Stamford Bridge. During a Christmas Day match against Portsmouth, he promptly scored four goals. Then came five goals against Wolves, the same versus West Bromwich, four against Newcastle and, in his last Chelsea game, four against Nottingham Forest. Add to those nine hat-tricks and his total in 169 games for Chelsea

stood at 132. Jimmy became the youngest player ever to score 100 League goals.

Although enjoying his football, he asked for a move from Chelsea as he thought they were not going anywhere. He got his move but it was an ill-fated transfer to AC Milan, and life in Italy was not to Greaves' liking. Although he scored 9 goals in 10 matches, he was not happy, and arguments within the club saw Jimmy on the transfer list. It was Bill Nicholson who stepped in to bring Greaves to White Hart Lane for £99,999. Jimmy had been only four months with Milan. Now at the club he supported as a youngster, he continued his record of scoring in his first game for a new club, but this time it happened at Plymouth Argyle for Spurs' reserves, as his League clearance was slow in coming through. The next week he scored a hat-trick against Blackpool in his senior Tottenham debut. It was the season after Tottenham's 'double' success and they went on to retain the FA Cup beating Burnley in the final, and then win the European Cup-Winners' Cup in 1963.

Jimmy was now a permanent fixture in the England team and popping the goals in as regular as before, plus enjoying his football once again. Everyone wanted Greaves in their team; Young England, the Football League XI and the Under-23s. He had made his first full England appearance versus Peru in 1959, and by the time he had appeared for his country 15 times

Jimmy Greaves in typical goal poaching mode as he slides the ball into the net at White Hart Lane in 1965.

he had produced 16 goals; a remarkable record. Greaves was at White Hart Lane for eight great seasons and he was top of the list of goalscorers each season, setting a League record as he did so. His biggest disappointment came in 1966 when he was dropped by Sir Alf Ramsey and was not in the England team who won the World Cup for their first and only time so far. Greaves had been struck down with jaundice in the 1965/66 season, which took away a lot of his strength, but he had recovered and had been at his best again for England in a match against Norway, netting four goals in a 6–1 victory. This was quite a shame for a player of Greaves' stature, who could win a game with just one second of genius.

Two of his Tottenham goals will stand in the Spurs supporters' minds forever. One against Leicester City, when he ghosted past several opponents before slipping the ball past Peter Shilton, and another of the same quality against Manchester United, when he finally went round the goalkeeper to pass the ball into the net, leaving the defence scattered. The last lap of Greaves' career came when he joined West Ham United during 1970, in a deal which saw Martin Peters join Tottenham.

Greaves announced his retirement the next season, in 1971, at the still-early age of thirty-one. In Spurs colours he had represented England on 42 occasions and scored 28 goals. A crowd of over 45,000 came to say goodbye to Greaves in October 1972 and he reminded everyone of why he was the champion by scoring the first goal in the match versus Feyenoord. Jimmy then made a brand new career for himself as a TV pundit, author and newspaper columnist.

Arthur Grimsdell
Half-back 1911-1929

	Appearances	Goals
League	324	26
FA Cup	36	1
Wartime	9	0
Other	48	11
TOTAL	417	

Many older Spurs supporters point to Arthur Grimsdell as the most complete footballer ever to grace the White Hart Lane ground, and his name will always come forward when trying to compare the great Tottenham teams of various eras. Of more recent footballers, Grimsdell could be likened to the legendary late Duncan Edwards of Manchester United fame. He was born in Watford, where he attended Watford Field School, and later joined his nearest club, Watford St Stephens, where his local senior club Watford spotted him. As a schoolboy he had always played at centre forward and had already been selected in that position for the England Schoolboys team. However, Watford saw in him more potential as a centre half and that was partly why Tottenham Hotspur acquired his services in 1909 as a fifteen-year-old schoolboy, having been the youngest player to have represented Watford Boys. He also was a more than adequate cricketer with Hertfordshire and he was said to have a career in that sport if he so desired.

His first game with Spurs was at the tail end of the 1911/12 season, at home to Bolton Wanderers on 20 April 1912, still only eighteen years of age, and he kept his place for the next match, the last of that season. Spurs played him at centre half at first but moved him to left half, a position he made his own for most of his years at White Hart Lane. At the age of just nineteen Arthur was on the brink of the England XI when he took part in the international trial match in November 1913, but his chance was put on ice when there came along the First World War.

Grimsdell was one of the first Tottenham footballers to volunteer for duty in the First World War and he missed three complete seasons during the conflict. He returned in 1919 and soon demonstrated he was stronger than ever. He was appointed captain of Spurs and received the FA Cup for Tottenham in 1921 when they beat Wolverhampton Wanderers 1-0 at Stamford Bridge. In April 1919 he took part in another international trial match for the

Arthur Grimsdelll in the centre, flanked by two other Tottenham Hotspur greats, Bert Bliss (right) and Jimmy Cantrell.

England team, and then a Victory International versus Scotland. In this game he showed his true form and scored two goals.

Grimsdell was captain of Tottenham right up to his retirement. It was his tireless displays that saw him form a fine left-wing triangle at White Hart Lane, together with Bert Bliss and the young Jimmy Dimmock, and the international selectors thought so too when all three were in the England team against Scotland at one time. Only injuries kept Grimsdell out of the Spurs team for the next few seasons, and he also played for England on six occasions between 1919 and 1923. He had developed into a strong but fair player, and led Spurs to the Second Division championship in 1920, scoring 14 goals as his shots from long range nearly always found the target. Not to say that he didn't shine in defence; he could always be seen battling away in the Spurs' final third of the pitch, and also shouting encouragement and orders to his fellow team

mates. Virtually all his matches with Spurs were at left half but with the odd flurry at left-back and centre half.

With Spurs standing on top of the League, Grimsdell suffered a broken leg at Leicester City on 31 October 1925, Tottenham losing the game 5-3, and he was out of the game for a long period, his comeback being on 30 April 1927 at Liverpool. It was now evident he had lost a lot of his strength and power and struggled to recapture his old form. His last season was 1928/29, in which he only played 11 matches, and Spurs decided to let him go, his Tottenham Hotspur career having spanned the years 1911 to 1929. Arthur joined Clapton Orient as player-manager, but a year later he was coaching schoolboys. Later on he had a sports shop at Romford, and was a director of Watford from 1945 to 1951. Altogether he scored 38 goals in his 417 appearances for Tottenham.

Willie Hall
Inside forward 1932-1944

	Appearances	Goals
League	204	27
FA Cup	20	2
Wartime	133	10
Other	18	6
TOTAL	375	

Every decade brought its own Spurs stars, and Willie Hall was shining throughout the thirties and even into the early forties. Born in Newark, Nottinghamshire, on 12 March 1912, he stood out while still a young schoolboy and was selected for the Nottinghamshire Schools team. He was playing at centre forward at that time and his remarkable skills soon won him a place in his works team Ransome & Marles. Soon Notts County heard about him and signed him in November 1930, and in his first season at Meadow Lane they became champions of the Third Division (South).

Two seasons later Tottenham brought him to White Hart Lane, playing him at inside left, his best position, and he played his first game for Spurs away at his former club Notts County. Although standing at only 5ft 7in, he was strongly built and as an inside forward he was very clever in linking defence with attack. By the end of the 1932/33 season he had helped lift Tottenham into the First Division, and the following season he was an ever-present in the side when they finished in third spot in the First Division.

Within a year of joining Spurs he made his England debut versus France, in December 1933, but four more years passed before he was awarded his second cap, and in that time Spurs had been relegated to the Second Division once more. Hall was a last-minute choice for the Football League versus the Irish League in 1937 and was in such great form that he was recalled to the England team shortly afterwards; he went on to make ten appearances for England. Although not renowned as a goalscorer, he hit the back of the net nine times for his country. At international level he formed a great right wing with Stanley Matthews and in the match against Ireland at Old Trafford, in November 1938, England won 7-0. Willie was in fine form for this encounter and scored five of the England goals. This burst came in a period of twenty-eight minutes and included possibly the fastest ever hat-trick in international football.

After this feat he said that he owed much to Matthews and Tommy Lawton who provided him with opportunities to score and added, 'My luck was in when I scored my fourth goal, I was back to the goal when I hooked the ball over my shoulder and it went in.' In 1938 Willie scored seven times for England but only five for Spurs.

War came along in 1939 and straightaway Hall, who was then captain of Tottenham, joined the War Police Reserve together with twelve other Spurs players, and he was known to all the staff from then on as PC372. When regional leagues were sorted out he was soon back where he was at his best, on a football pitch. Even when Spurs had a vacant Saturday he went to Upton Park and played for West Ham for one game, this being the only time he played as a guest for any other side. Throughout the early years of the war he was ready and willing to play in any position wanted, and on one occasion was even getting the goalkeeper's jersey on until the Tottenham goalkeeper arrived at the last minute.

Early in 1943 Hall began to have trouble with a foot problem, and the following March he confirmed that he was retiring from football and would not be putting on the famous white shirt anymore. He had played 133 wartime matches for Tottenham, his last game being against Crystal Palace on 27 November 1943. It was a serious leg disease that had struck Willie down and sadly he soon had to have one leg amputated, then both legs below the knee. Spurs played a benefit match versus an FA side at White Hart Lane on Tuesday 7 May 1946, and Willie sat near the tunnel as the teams came out and shook hands with all of them. His heart was still in football and he joined Clapton Orient as a coach, then manager, between September and November 1945. Following spells as manager of Chelmsford City, and then Chingford, he found his disability too much, and he was licensee of a public house in east London for a while. After 375 appearances for Spurs, with 45 goals to his credit, he passed away at Newark on 22 May 1967.

Willie Hall leading Spurs out in 1936, with a determined look on his face.

Tommy Harmer

Inside forward 1948-1960

	Appearances	Goals
League	205	47
FA Cup	17	4
Other	51 (2)	18
TOTAL	275	

Tommy Harmer was an entertainer and footballer of the highest calibre, with 100 per cent control of the football and many tricks up his sleeve. But for all this he was never a permanent member of the Tottenham team, except for one period in the late 1950s. He was born 2 February 1928 in Hackney, east London, and at his best stood just 5ft 6in in height and weighed only 8st 9lbs. It was right at the back end of the Second World War that Harmer began to appear on the Tottenham scene. He was picked out as one with skill and determination and was in the Spurs Juniors reserve side, scoring five goals in one match. The club was not sure, however, if his slight frame and build would manage to survive in the rigours of competitive football. They signed him on amateur forms in 1945 and he was loaned out to Finchley for a while.

Harmer became a Spurs professional in August 1948 and was an ever-present in the Spurs 'A' team and the reserves in consecutive seasons. He had to wait until 8 September 1951 to make his competitive first-team debut against Bolton Wanderers at White Hart Lane, although he had been unwrapped on 1 May 1950 when he made an appearance against Hibernian in a friendly. Tommy played one game for England 'B' in 1952 and had several outings in the FA XI. He continued to make spasmodic appearances during the next few seasons but came into his own in 1956/57 when he became the main playmaker in the Tottenham side, playing in all 51 matches that season, snapping up twenty goals in the process. He missed just two games in the following campaign, scoring another nine goals, while penalties became his speciality, which he took with all his revered artistry. When Bill Nicholson became manager, the team celebrated with a 10-4 victory over Everton and it was said that Tommy Harmer scored one goal and made the other nine.

Despite missing only five games in 1959/60, he did not figure in Nicholson's plans and he missed out on the next few glory years. He moved to Watford in October 1960 and ended his career at Chelsea, playing six games and then coaching, until retiring in June 1967. His 275 games at Tottenham produced 69 goals, but how many more did he create?

Ron Henry
Full-back 1954-1967

	Appearances	Goals
League	247	1
FA Cup	23	0
Europe	17	0
Other	51 (4)	1
TOTAL	342	

A one-club man throughout his career, Ron Henry was born in Shoreditch, London, on 17 August 1934, but was brought up at Redbourne in Hertfordshire which he considered his home. After playing for Harpenden Schools and Hertfordshire Schools, he was offered a trial by Wolverhampton Wanderers, but this was cancelled and he heard nothing further so he signed amateur forms for Luton Town. He was playing at outside left at this time, but during his National Service days, stationed at Woolwich, he converted to left half and began playing with Harpenden Town and Redbourne.

After signing for Tottenham as an amateur in 1954, he stepped up to the professional ranks in January 1955, making his first appearance in Spurs colours on 12 April 1955 against Huddersfield Town at centre half. This was his only match in that season but he was consistent, as he played just one match in each of the next two seasons, both at left-back, the position that he had settled into. Ron had to wait until halfway through the 1959/60 season to make the no.3 shirt his own, and he was then an ever-present in the 'double' season; in the period from 28 November 1959 to 31 August 1963 he missed only one game.

It was in the 1961 FA Cup final against Leicester City that Henry showed what a key member of the Spurs side he was, being Man of the Match for most people, his solid defending giving nothing away. Many critics then asked why he had not been picked for England; this honour came along in February 1963 against France, in Alf Ramsey's first game as England manager. Unfortunately France won 5-1 and Ron was not selected after this. Not renowned as a goalscorer, he scored his one and only League goal against Manchester United, a long drive from over thirty yards that found the net of the eventual champions, giving Tottenham a 1-0 win.

As a reward for his loyalty and consistent play, he was given the captaincy of Spurs following Blanchflower's retirement, being in this post until a troublesome injury ended his first-team appearances. He dropped down to the reserves, then coached the 'A' side and the juniors at White Hart Lane. Altogether Ron had sixteen years playing for Spurs, playing in 342 senior games, and was a Spurs stalwart through and through.

Glenn Hoddle
Midfield 1975-1987

	Appearances	Goals
League	371 (7)	88
FA Cup	47 (1)	11
League Cup	44	10
Europe	17 (4)	1
Other	88 (11)	22
TOTAL	590	

Glenn Hoddle was a player in the true Tottenham Hotspur mode, and one of the modern greats of White Hart Lane. He was a player you either liked or who made you tear your hair out, there was no in between; even the England bosses during his time were not altogether sure of how or where to play him in the side. In fact, he was the type of player that a national team should have been fashioned around. Glenn was born in Hayes, in Middlesex, on 27 October 1957, and started out on his glittering career with junior side Spinney Dynamos. It was after moving to Harlow that he was selected for Harlow Schools, followed by the Essex Schools, and Martin Chives, who was presenting the prizes in a local junior cup final, recommended Glenn to Tottenham.

Hoddle became an apprentice at Spurs in April 1974 and quickly moved through the ranks, despite suffering a quite serious leg injury in his teens; he was upgraded a year later

to professional status. He was already picking up England Youth caps and in his early days at White Hart Lane he soon added England Under-21 and England 'B' appearances to his collection. He had sublime touch and vision, and often his teammates were not thinking along the same lines; this led to some arguments about him being a luxury in any side. In his first full season with Tottenham they were relegated, but he still shone brightly for Spurs, even in their one season in the Second Division, missing just one game as they fought their way back to the top flight. It seems strange even now to imagine Hoddle playing in the Second Division, but he played his part, scoring 13 goals from midfield.

It was during Terry Neill's short time as Spurs manager that Hoddle was given his chance to prove his worth and he made his debut on 30 August 1975, coming on as substitute at home to Norwich City. Before this season had finished he had shown his true worth at Stoke City in a 2-1 victory, with a splendid goal from distance beating England's Peter Shilton. One of his best goals was every schoolboy's dream, as he ran nearly the length of the pitch brushing aside opponents before sending the Oxford goalkeeper the wrong way with a shrug of the shoulders before sliding the ball in the net.

He made his England debut versus Bulgaria

Glenn Hoddle brings the ball under control after a not-so-good pass from a colleague v. Wolves at White Hart Lane.

in 1979, marking this with a goal, going on to win 44 England caps in his time with Tottenham. Many said that the England XI should have been built around Hoddle, but no-one was seemingly brave enough to take up the suggestion. In the 1979/80 season he was Spurs top scorer with 23 to his name, and in 1980 he was voted the PFA Young Player of the Year. With Hoddle it was not all about him dribbling round almost everyone on the pitch and scoring a goal each time. He was lucky to have around him at Tottenham other players of skill and thought, who were nearly always tuned in to his wavelength, and many goals arrived via his artistry.

In his 590 games with Tottenham he collected 132 goals, also winning FA Cup medals in 1981 and 1982, when he scored in both the final and the replay. He also played in the 1982 Football League Cup final and the FA Cup final in 1987, but missed out in the 1984 UEFA Cup victory when he was injured. After thirteen years at Tottenham, he went to Monaco for a £750,000 fee; who knows what he would be worth in today's much inflated prices. He helped them to the French League title in 1988 and was voted the best foreign player in the League.

His old serious knee trouble then flared up and in 1990 he bought up his contract and returned to England, where he linked up with Chelsea on a non-contract basis, but never played for them. In March 1991 he joined Swindon Town as player-manager, as a replacement for Ardiles, who had moved on. Hoddle soon had his new team playing in his style, while he himself reverted to a more defensive role. Later on he was given the top job of England manager, but after some success was relieved of his post, based on his thoughts put into words. He became manager at Southampton and then went back to his roots at White Hart Lane. This time it did not work and he left in early 2003. He became Wolverhampton Wanderers' manager the next season.

Mel Hopkins
Full-back 1952-1964

	Appearances	Goals
League	219	0
FA Cup	20	0
Europe	1	0
Other	31	1
TOTAL	271	

Born on 7 November 1934 in the Rhondda Valley, Wales, Mel was spotted by both Tottenham Hotspur and Manchester United when playing for the Ystrad Boys Club and both clubs invited him to join their ground staff. He chose Spurs, mainly because other youngsters from that area had decided on the London club. A Spurs amateur in May 1951, he moved up to full-time professional in May 1952, and continued to progress quite rapidly. Within six months he had made the breakthrough into the senior side, making his debut versus Derby County, away, on 12 October 1952, when he was just seventeen. However, he stepped in only as a replacement for either Willis or Withers, who were still holding the full-back positions at the time.

In the mid-1950s he was looked upon as one of the finest full-backs in the country, playing his first match for Wales in April 1956

and keeping his place from then on. Though an attacking full-back, Mel only scored once for Spurs, this coming in an Anglo-Scottish floodlit competition in 1956 against Hibernian, which was drawn 3-3. When the 'double' season came along, he had unfortunately just lost his place in the Tottenham line-up because of a broken nose sustained when playing for Wales at Hampden Park, and he did not play any senior games that historic season. He was still the automatic choice for his country; his best international season for Wales included the World Cup of 1958 in Sweden, when they qualified against all odds for the finals. Hopkins was outstanding and his best match was up against the genius of Garrincha, when he gave a faultless display.

Back at White Hart Lane his appearances for the first team were stuttering to say the least, and he played his last match in a Spurs shirt versus Ipswich Town on 4 April 1964. Having won 34 caps for Wales, Hopkins moved to Brighton & Hove Albion in October 1964 and played his part in their Fourth Division championship victory. He later appeared for Ballymena and Canterbury, and joined his last club, Bradford Park Avenue, in January 1969. Mel then became a sports instructor and also a sports officer at the Horsham Sports Centre. Altogether he made 271 appearances for Tottenham Hotspur.

David Howells
Midfield 1985-1998

	Appearances	Goals
League	238 (39)	22
FA Cup	17 (4)	1
League Cup	26 (5)	4
Europe	6	0
Other	36 (3)	4
TOTAL	374	

Loyal to Tottenham throughout most of his career, Howells made his debut for the club, as a centre forward, at Sheffield Wednesday on 22 February 1986, scoring the winning goal. His next game, the following season, was at outside right, but his position left him free to make his mark anywhere on the playing field. At nearly 6ft in height he was always a fine header of the ball, and although playing most of his matches in midfield, he often surprised everyone with his advances upfield at set-pieces. Howells was born in Guildford, Surrey, in December 1967, and came to Spurs' notice when in the Surrey Schools team. In July 1984 he joined Tottenham under the Youth Training Scheme and became a professional six months later.

He was selected for the England Youths as a centre forward, then the Under-19 team, but at White Hart Lane manager Terry Venables moved David into midfield, where his skill as a fine reader of the game would stand him in good stead. This was where he began to flourish and he soon came to be quite a regular in the side as an all-rounder of fine ability; by the early 1990s he let nobody down with his consistent performances for Tottenham. The match at Nottingham Forest in October 1990 shows only too well his contribution to Spurs: Forest went ahead only for Howells to curl in an equaliser. Moments later he was back in defence, clearing a goal-bound shot from off the goal line, and he was not done yet as he strode forward to head home Spurs' winning goal.

He deserved more recognition in the England representative side after his early performances for the young England sides, but this was not to be, and he continued to give 100 per cent to Tottenham Hotspur. He often played as an anchor when Gascoigne was in his most attacking modes, frequently plugging the gaps when the Spurs superstar made his bursts up-field. Howells was a member of the Tottenham FA Cup winning side of 1991 and was his usual versatile self on the big stage of Wembley Stadium. Following fourteen years at White Hart Lane, David joined Southampton in July 1998 after 374 appearances and 31 goals for Tottenham

	Appearances	Goals
League	293 (4)	12
FA Cup	34 (2)	1
League Cup	33 (2)	2
Europe	29 (1)	4
Other	96 (5)	3
TOTAL	499	

Born in Forest Gate in east London on 11 December 1958, Chris had a twelve-year career at White Hart Lane. He qualified to play for the Republic of Ireland through his mother's side – she came from Limerick; his father was West Indian. He made his first appearance in the green shirt in October 1979, and went on to gain 53 international caps. He was also an important member of the Republic's successful European Championship squad in 1988, and in the World Cup of 1990. Tottenham spotted him in junior football after he had played for Newnham Schools, but he only signed on part-time in May 1977 as he wanted to complete his apprenticeship as a lift engineer.

Chris turned full-time professional in June 1979 and made his League debut on 29 August that year in the Football League Cup against Manchester United at White Hart Lane. He then went on to play in the remainder of the Spurs matches that season at right or left-back, scoring one goal against Brighton & Hove Albion. Chris was almost an ever-present for

Spurs from then onwards. He suffered an injury part-way through the 1980/81 season, but he recovered to regain his place and won an FA Cup winners' medal in 1981 and 1982, and he was in the Spurs UEFA Cup winning side in 1984. Chris was also a member of the Spurs runners-up teams in the Football League Cup in 1982 and the 1987 FA Cup.

In his early days Hughton had played on the wing, and he was one of the most attacking full-backs of the modern football game. Although a natural right-footed player, Hughton preferred to play on the left-hand side; this did not stop him showing his dexterity and thoughtful distribution of the ball when playing forward.

After twelve years of fine service to Spurs, Hughton was given a free transfer in 1990, and he moved to West Ham on loan, quickly making it permanent. He helped them gain promotion to the First Division in 1990/91 and then joined Brentford for just one season when a knee injury saw him retire. He appeared back at White Hart Lane in 1993, serving on the coaching staff and looking after the reserves and the Under-21 side. Chris is also on the management staff of the Republic of Ireland. He scored 22 goals in 499 games for Tottenham.

George Hunt
Centre forward 1930-1937

	Appearances	Goals
League	185	125
FA Cup	13	13
Other	7	13
TOTAL	205	

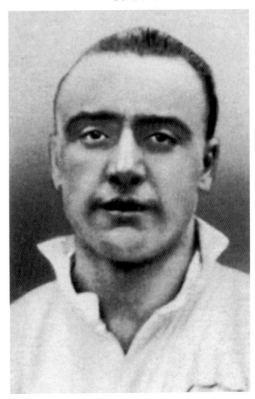

Seven seasons at White Hart Lane saw George Hunt consistently scoring from 1930 to 1937. His record at Tottenham stood at 151 goals from 205 appearances – one of the best averages of any Spurs centre forward. This came after his debut on 20 September 1930, and then a long break before he was selected for the senior side again, towards the end of that season, but he scored 8 times in 11 outings, including a hat-trick in the London FA Charity Cup semi-final win of 8-1 over Ilford. Season 1931/32 saw Hunt firmly positioned at centre forward in the Spurs team and he was top marksman with 26 goals, going on to record 36 the next season and 38 in 1933/34. This remained the record for many years, until the time of Bobby Smith. In this period Tottenham tried to confuse matters in two of the seasons, when Douglas Hunt arrived at White Hart Lane and shared the centre forward position with George Hunt. During his spell at Spurs George helped them back into the First Division, although they slipped back again after two years. George Hunt was a ball-playing type of leader and caught the eye of the England selectors, gaining three caps when with Spurs. His skills in beating an opponent invited defenders to tackle hard and he suffered several injuries, but he still persisted in playing the game the only way he knew how.

He was born in Barnsley on 22 February 1910 and was playing for Regent Street Congregationals when he had trials with Port Vale, Sheffield United and Barnsley, none of whom decided to take him on board, to their regret. Chesterfield signed him in 1929, but after one season of notching a hatful of goals, Tottenham stepped in to bring him to White Hart Lane, in June 1930, and he was manager Percy Smith's best signing. When Smith left, George was left out of the team for long spells and he moved to Arsenal in October 1937, after signing off his Spurs career with both goals in a 2-1 win over Nottingham Forest on 27 March 1937. After only six months at Highbury, and three goals, he was on his way to Bolton Wanderers. He was a regular for the Lancashire side throughout the Second World War, and retired after two years at Sheffield Wednesday, returning to Bolton as coach when he retired in 1948, a post he held for twenty years. He then left football for a job in a garage in Bolton.

Pat Jennings MBE ————————————————

Goalkeeper 1964-1977, 1983-1986

	Appearances	Goals
League	473	0
FA Cup	43	0
League Cup	39	0
Europe	36	0
Other	82 (3)	1
TOTAL	676	

Born in Newry in County Down on 12 June 1945, Pat is truly one of the great legends of Tottenham Hotspur. His first period with the club was from 1964 to 1977, returning in 1983, having been forgiven for moving to Arsenal for a spell. At his best Jennings was the best goalkeeper in the world, and Spurs' older supporters, who saw both Ditchburn and Jennings, will continue to wonder which was the best goalkeeper for Tottenham Hotspur. Pat started out playing Gaelic football for North Down School, but switched to football on leaving school and joined junior side Newry United. After a year and a half he moved to Newry Town and he was soon on the move up the soccer ladder. Ex-Irish international Bill McClacken recommended him to Watford, whose manager Ron Burgess watched him play for Northern Ireland in a youth tournament at Bognor Regis in 1963, and straightaway signed him for £6,000. He was selected for the Watford First XI immediately, quickly showing one of his great assets of a large pair of hands for one so young.

After just a season, playing 52 matches and being a magnet for some of the top clubs, nineteen-year-old Pat joined Tottenham in June 1964 for £27,000, probably one of the best bargains of all time made by manager Bill Nicholson. Brought to White Hart Lane to take over from Bill Brown, the first two seasons saw both of them fighting it out for the first team place. It was in the Tottenham FA Cup winning season of 1966/67 that Jennings became the permanent goalkeeper for Spurs, playing in 50 of the club's 51 matches, and he had definitely come to stay. On the field he gave the impression of being in complete control, which spread to his teammates, who had confidence in the 6ft figure between the Spurs goalposts. Before the matches he did show a little sign of being nervous, but this soon disappeared as he became a fixture for Spurs. His large hands made it seem he had glue on them when he reached out to pluck the ball from an attacker's head, but this attribute was not the sole sum of his talent; he would use legs, knees and anything else to stop goal-bound shots. Jennings was also able to jump higher than many goalkeepers. Opposing sides would put crosses into the Spurs' defence, only to see a large gloved hand pluck the ball, often one-handed, out of the air.

It was in the FA Charity Shield of 1967 at

Jennings saves the second of two penalties at Anfield.

Old Trafford that Jennings produced a moment to treasure, clearing the ball upfield only to see the Manchester United goalkeeper misjudge the bounce of the mighty clearance; he could only watch as the ball went over his head into the net. There have been goals scored by goalkeepers before, from penalties or free kicks, but this was scored in open play. There are many Jennings moments to recall, such as saving two penalties in one match at Anfield; Liverpool's Keegan and Tommy Smith being the two players denied. During his first and best spell at White Hart Lane, Pat helped Spurs win four trophies and run up the appearance record for the club, 673, since beaten by Steve Perryman.

The Football Writers' Player of the Year award came Jennings' way in 1972/73 and he was voted the Professional Footballers Association Player of the Year in the season 1975/76. On top of this came the MBE for services to the game in the Queen's Birthday Honours of 1976. In November 1976 Jennings was given a testimonial match versus Arsenal. He had been lucky in injuries for most of his career, but Pat did sustain a rather bad ankle injury in 1976/77 and missed many games, this being the relegation year at Tottenham.

In August 1977 Pat was let go to Arsenal, where in an eight-year stay he won another FA Cup winners' medal, then made his farewell appearance for Ireland in the World Cup of 1986, this being his 119th cap for his country. He was, by then, back at Spurs for a second spell. His role was as a standby goalkeeper and he played one match in the Screen Sport Super Cup against Liverpool. He now plays his part in the corporate hospitality at White Hart Lane. His appearances for Tottenham totalled 676.

Cliff Jones
Winger 1957-1968

	Appearances	Goals
League	314 (4)	135
FA Cup	35 (4)	16
League Cup	2	1
Europe	19	7
Other	38 (2)	17
TOTAL	418	

Cliff Jones was another from the Principality of Wales to make his name at White Hart Lane. He had been born into a football family; his father Ivor was a Wales international, his brother Bryn was with Swansea and Bournemouth, while an uncle of the same name moved from Wolves to Arsenal before the Second World War for a British record fee. Cliff was born in Swansea on 7 February 1935 and, like many others, first came to prominence for Swansea Schools and then for the Welsh Schoolboys, before joining his local team Swansea, first part-time and then in May 1952 as a professional.

Tottenham Hotspur had to pay a £35,000 fee to bring him to White Hart Lane in February 1958, at the time when he was a private in the army, serving at the barracks at St Johns Wood in London. He took a time to settle down at Spurs and this was not helped when he suffered a hairline fracture of the leg in training. He had already played for Wales while at Swansea, and his debut for Tottenham was in a 4-4 draw at Highbury on 22 February 1958, in which he did not have a very good game. After his injury he did not reappear until December 1958, when he began to show the form he was capable of; his speedy winding runs at the opponents' defence saw him clipped down as they could not outwit him. In fact, in the 'double' year of 1961, Jones played the least out of the recognised team, appearing in just 29 League matches. A winger who favoured the left wing although a natural right-footed player, standing only 5ft 7in, he scored many goals with his head with some spring-heeled jumps over the defence, and is remembered for the way he often left his marker with a fine burst of speed.

Cliff was the last member of the 1961 'super' Spurs side to move from Tottenham, going to Fulham for a cut price £5,000 in October 1968, leaving his record of 418 appearances and 176 goals, the last being in his final Spurs match against Manchester United. He only played 25 matches at Fulham, scoring 2 goals, and from 1970 he had short periods in non-League circles at Kings Lynn, Bedford, Wealdstone and Cambridge City, ending as player-coach with Wingate. He is often seen back at White Hart Lane at some function or other when the older players are in evidence.

Ledley King
Defender 1997-

	Appearances	Goals
League	146	3
FA Cup	13	2
League Cup	10	1
TOTAL	169	

Although still playing at White Hart Lane, Ledley has fast become a firm favourite amongst Tottenham supporters, and stands up well against some great Spurs players of the past. He was born at Bow in the east of London on 12 October 1980 and attended the Blessed John Roche School at Poplar. He played for London Schools and Tower Hamlets before becoming a member of the Leyton Orient Centre of Excellence. He first signed for Tottenham on associated schoolboy terms in February 1996, and progressed to the juniors, making 18 appearances with them and one outing for the Spurs senior youth side in 1996/97. Ledley was added to the trainee staff at Spurs, and was already an England Under-16 international. He was then upgraded to the professional ranks in July 1998 and won six caps for the England Under-17 side.

He made his League debut versus Liverpool at Anfield on 1 May 1999, coming on as a substitute, and was not overawed by the surroundings. During the following season of 1999/2000 he had three more League outings plus a seat on the substitutes' bench on a further six occasions. He settled down as a central defender, which seems to be his best position, although he can also play well in midfield positions. Still collecting honours, Ledley was an England Youth player as well as playing in the Under-21 side for England, steadily moving upwards through the ranks.

He became a regular in the Tottenham Premier Reserve League side and was one of the younger players looked to for the future of Spurs, shown when he made a further 23 appearances in the first team the next season. He was on the scoresheet for the first time when his goal, ten seconds in, at Bradford City on 9 December 2000 created a Premiership record. To date, Ledley has held down a regular place in the Spurs line-up and has begun to force his way into the full England side, including in the European Championship in 2004, when he was drafted into the most important match of the tournament against the strong side of France, in which he was Man of the Match. Long may the supporters see King in action at White Hart Lane.

Joe Kinnear
Full-back 1965-1975

	Appearances	Goals
League	190 (7)	2
FA Cup	24	0
League Cup	20	0
Europe	18	0
Other	40 (3)	4
TOTAL	302	

Joe was a real favourite at Tottenham for around twelve years, and is always welcomed back when he appears with his team of the moment. He was born in Dublin on 27 December 1947 but moved to England with his family when he was seven years old, and settled in Hertfordshire. Joe was soon playing for Watford Schools and then being made captain of Hertfordshire Schoolboys. When no League team offered him a contract he settled down to play for St Albans City, and it was then that Tottenham saw the potential in him; he joined them in 1963, signing as a professional in February 1965.

Only two months passed before he made his debut at right-back against West Ham United on 8 April 1966, Spurs having tried five players in that position, and Joe held on to that no.2 shirt for the rest of the season. The next season he suffered an injury halfway through the season but recovered to win an FA Cup winners' medal against Chelsea. Football League Cup winners' medals also came his way in 1971 and 1973.

Joe's big breakthrough to play for his country, the Republic of Ireland, came in February 1967

against Turkey and he went on to play for his country on 25 occasions. As a quick, hardworking defender he formed a fine partnership at Spurs with Cyril Knowles, overlapping to turn up as another attacker, but he never lost sight of his job in defence. Kinnear picked up his share of injuries, and the worst one saw him suffer a broken leg in two places; he had to sit out for the best part of a year.

His appearances for Spurs were gradually reducing when he was recalled to play an important part in Tottenham's successful struggle to avoid relegation in the 1974/75 season. This was to be Joe's swansong and in the summer of 1975 he moved to Brighton, where Spurs played a testimonial match for him. He retired and stepped into management at Doncaster Rovers, but joined Wimbledon as manager when they had a grand spell after being voted into the Football League. A period of ill health followed before he was back in football at Luton and then Nottingham Forest. His matches for Spurs total 302 scoring 6 goals.

Jurgen Klinsmann
Striker 1994-1995, 1998

	Appearances	Goals
League	56	29
FA Cup	9	5
League Cup	3	4
Other	4	3
TOTAL	72	

Spurs pulled off what is thought to be the most superb transfer sensation of all time when they swooped out of the blue to sign Germany's Jurgen Klinsmann from Monaco in August 1994. Spurs had just been handed a fine of £1.5 million for irregular cash dealings, as well as being docked six points for the coming 1994/95 season, and were excluded from the FA Cup for one year. Some hard talking was done to entice Klinsmann to White Hart Lane, much of this coming from Alan Sugar on his yacht in the south of France. The Tottenham fans needed something to cheer about and this happened when the news arrived that Klinsmann, the top player in Europe, possibly the world, was to play at White Hart Lane.

His debut, in a friendly at Watford on 6 August, saw the largest crowd ever turn out to see the new boy at Spurs. His first goal for Tottenham came in another friendly, this time at little Shelbourne, and he was up and running; the price quoted for the German to top the scoring list was 12-1, an interesting flutter. Klinsmann then went on to score the winning goal in the first League match at Sheffield Wednesday, the result being 4-3. He showed he had a sense of humour by diving across the turf alongside other Spurs players to celebrate his goal – a reference to his reputation for diving to win free-kicks and penalties. This celebration was reprised just a few times during the rest of the season, as he thought the other clubs' supporters would not be so happy about it.

Spurs had a great season, as the ban on the FA Cup was lifted, as well as the six-point deduction, and Tottenham reached the semi-final of the FA Cup, bringing millions back to watch football, especially when Klinsmann was on view. In 50 games for Spurs he scored 29 goals. It was a surprise when Jurgen decided to move on from Spurs after one season, and he returned to Germany and Bayern Munich, then Sampdoria.

In the 1997/98 season Spurs were fighting hard to avert the drop from the Premier League and something was needed to spur them to avoid relegation. It came in the figure of Jurgen Klinsmann, who returned in January 1998 to try and work miracles, which happened as he was the Spurs' top scorer with nine goals, including four at Wimbledon in a 6-2 victory, and Tottenham were safe again. Overall at Spurs, Klinsmann scored 41 times in his 72 appearances.

Cyril Knowles
Full-back 1964-1977

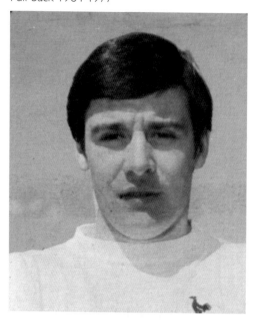

	Appearances	Goals
League	401 (1)	15
FA Cup	42	1
League Cup	32 (1)	0
Europe	30	1
Other	62	3
TOTAL	569	

'Nice One Cyril' is the pop song written about a certain footballer that entered the pop charts in 1973, and for twelve years the voices of the Spurs supporters swelled around the White Hart Lane stadium as he became a cult figure. His own personal song also became a widespread catchphase as well. Even now, when fans are asked to name some of their favourite Tottenham Hotspur players of yesteryear, Cyril Knowles' name will figure well to the fore. He was an excellent full-back who was unlucky to gain only four full caps for England, against Russia, Spain, Sweden and West Germany, all in 1967/68. Knowles was born on 13 July 1944 at Fitzwilliam in Yorkshire, the same village that produced cricketer Geoff Boycott. Cyril's brother Peter Knowles was also a fine footballer with Wolverhampton Wanderers, before taking up a religious occupation. Cyril was an outside left in his schooldays at South Emshall School, joining Manchester United for a year, playing for their 'A' team as a junior before being rejected. He carried on playing with his local club Hemsworth and working down the pit. He also turned to rugby for a while, before coming back to soccer with further spells at Blackpool

and Wolves, who also thought he wouldn't make the grade.

Then along came Middlesbrough, who saw something in his play and signed him on in October 1962, and he went on to become one of the best full-backs the club ever had. He made his debut for them in April 1963, and he soon attracted scouts from other top clubs, Bill Nicholson stepping in to bring him to White Hart Lane after just 39 appearances for Middlesbrough, for a fee of £45,000. For Cyril it was like stepping into a big new world, and he said afterwards that his best introduction to Spurs was a game of tennis with Dave Mackay.

Knowles played his first match for Tottenham in a friendly with Feyenoord in August 1964, but his Football League debut was against Sheffield United on 22 August 1964 at right-back. He went on to play in 43 matches that season and followed this by missing just one match the next season at left-back, where he settled down to claim the position for his own. Visions are often conjured up of his spirited overlapping runs, showing part of his earlier days as a winger, and his crosses were turned into goals from the heads

Not always content with a hefty clearance from defence, Knowles is shown here looking for a more helpful way to set Spurs on the attack.

of Chivers, Peters and Gilzean. Cyril was a born entertainer who enjoyed a fine rapport with the Spurs fans and with his skill and experience he gave his all for the Tottenham cause. From his second season onwards he was never absent from the Spurs line-up, except when nursing an injury. One of his best memories is the final game of the 1974/75 season and a game against Leeds, which Spurs had to win to avoid relegation; this they did with a Knowles double of a penalty and a free-kick.

Injuries began to affect him more and knee problems saw him miss five months; this eventually led to his early retirement from the game. He couldn't leave the game altogether and after a spell at Hertford Town he returned north as a scout for Spurs. After working as a coach he was appointed assistant manager at Middlesbrough in February 1982, before taking his first manager's job at Darlington from 1983 to 1987, where he led his team to promotion from the Fourth Division. He was an excellent manager who thrived on getting the best and more out of a club with very limited finance; he showed this when he took Torquay United to the Sherpa Van Trophy in 1989. Knowles was then appointed manager back in his homeland at Hartlepool United. He was manoeuvring them into a place for promotion in his first year in charge when a shattering diagnosis of a serious brain illness hit him, and he passed away six months later on 31 August 1991. He was mourned not just by the clubs he had been with, but by the entire football world. He appeared 569 times in the Spurs team and scored 20 goals.

Gary Lineker OBE

Striker 1989-1992

	Appearances	Goals
League	105	67
FA Cup	9	3
League Cup	16	8
Europe	8	2
Other	24 (3)	10
TOTAL	165	

One of the leading goalscorers in modern-day football, Gary Lineker's short three-year stay at Tottenham must be included on the basis that he is as well known as a Tottenham Hotspur great as for his seasons at Leicester City, Everton and Barcelona, where he built his reputation as a goalscorer of great prowess. He was born in Leicester on 30 November 1960, and it is with his home-town club that he made his early impression on the football world as a raw apprentice. Gary had to wait two years in the wings as a young professional until Leicester gave him his chance in the match versus Oldham Athletic on 1 January 1979. His seven appearances that season, and his one goal, did not really herald his career and it was not until the 1981/82 season that he gained a regular place in the team. He was in the successful Leicester side that won the Second Division Championship in 1980, and again in 1983.

By the time his home team let him move on to Everton he had reached his century of goals, and had already made his England debut against Scotland in May 1983. However, his new club only had the benefit of his talent for one season when he topped their scoring chart with 40 strikes in 57 matches. Following this with the 'golden boot' award at the World Cup in Mexico, he attracted the attention of Barcelona who paid out £2.75 million to take him to Spain for three years.

It was when Terry Venables left Spain to take the reins at Tottenham that Lineker arrived at White Hart Lane in 1989 for £1.2 million, to thrive on the skills of Gascoigne. Not all Gary's goals were firmly hit shots; he was always lurking in the area of the opponents' goalmouth for some tap-ins and some bundled goals, but they all counted. He was top scorer in each of his three years at Spurs and reached the total of 49 goals for England, also gaining an FA Cup winners' medal in 1991, still keeping his record of never being booked in his whole career. For his services to football he was awarded the OBE in 1992 and has thrived in a new role in the TV world. Appearances for Spurs were 165, which produced 90 goals.

George Ludford
Forward, half-back 1936-1950

	Appearances	Goals
League	77	7
FA Cup	6	1
Wartime	170	76
Other	22	7
TOTAL	275	

A shining example of a real club man, George spent twenty-four years with Tottenham, starting on the ground staff in May 1931, through to 1955, and then only moving a mile or so up the road to become manager of Enfield. He was born in Barnet, Hertfordshire, on 22 March 1915 and began to shine as a prolific goalscorer when in the Tottenham Juniors side for two years. Then he was sent, like so many other promising youngsters, to Spurs' nursery club Northfleet, where he continued to hit the net, including a golden season, 1935/36, when he scored 101 goals as a centre forward, a record which will be extremely hard to beat.

This sped up his elevation to the full professional ranks at White Hart Lane in May 1936, and he made his League debut at inside left against West Ham United, away, on 29 August 1936. This was his only match in that season and he didn't reappear until halfway through the following season, playing at centre forward against Manchester United at Old Trafford. It seems that he was not quite the finished article as, again, this was his only appearance, but the next season he played in 10 games, scoring 6 goals. George was also in a friendly match against Arsenal at Colchester, and when the 1939/40 season got underway he was in the Spurs side from the beginning. This only lasted three matches as the Second World War broke out and football was put on hold for a while.

Through the dark days Ludford joined the Police Reserve at Tottenham and managed to play 187 games for Spurs during the conflict; he was also second highest scorer with 81. As well as his appearances with Spurs, George helped out other clubs, including Reading, Southend, Fulham, Clapton Orient, Chelsea, Queens Park Rangers, West Ham and Millwall where he became quite a favourite, playing in their League Cup final side at Wembley. He was now at wing half for Spurs and when normal service was resumed he missed only one match in 1946/47, but he then found himself filling in wherever he could and did not really hold down a regular place.

He played his last game in the League versus Southampton at White Hart Lane on 25 February 1950, and for the next four years he was the steady influence in the reserve side until he retired in 1954, when he continued on the coaching staff. In his 275 appearances for Tottenham he scored 91 goals.

	Appearances	Goals
League	458 (19)	27
FA Cup	45 (2)	5
League Cup	60 (2)	2
Europe	22 (3)	4
Other	162 (23)	15
TOTAL	796	

An example to all youngsters who wanted to make football their career, Gary was diagnosed with diabetes in 1978 at the age of seventeen but he didn't let that get in the way of his favourite sport. Born in Bristol on 23 August 1961, he had football in his family; his father Ray played for Bristol Rovers and Newport County, while his brother Kevin was a striker with Bristol City and Crystal Palace. After playing for Bristol and Avon Schools, Gary joined Bristol Rovers, his father's team, as an apprentice, and he soon moved up to professional in January 1979. He had made his Football League debut for Bristol in December 1978 while still a young apprentice, and from then on he was virtually an ever-present for the Rovers, and built up a reputation of an extremely versatile player. He was selected in several different positions during his four years at Bristol and made 141 appearances before he moved to White Hart Lane in August 1982 for a £120,000 fee.

He had already been a regular in the England Youth side and had been selected for the England Under-21s on three occasions. Gary was certainly thrown in at the deep end when he was in the Tottenham side for the FA Charity Shield against Liverpool at Wembley in August 1982. He quickly began to show his versatility in his first season at Spurs, playing in six different positions, and also scoring ten goals along the way. He was the club's second highest scorer in the League, helping them to fourth place in the First Division for the second consecutive season. In his first League match for Tottenham he scored his first goal in the 2-2 draw against Luton Town at White Hart Lane. The 1984/85 season was a frustrating one for Mabbutt as he was named as a substitute in nearly half of his games, 13 in all, but from 1986 he was a regular, only injury saw him on the sidelines. He had settled down as a midfield player, which allowed his attacking and defensive skill to shine at all times, and his height of 5ft 9in was no barrier, as he seemed to posses a coiled spring in his boots. England boss Bobby Robson was so impressed with him, and his quick adaptation to the top flight, that he handed Gary his first full England cap against West Germany just two months after

Gary Mabbutt holds the FA Cup aloft after a victory over Nottingham Forest in 1991.

the player's arrival at White Hart Lane.

When David Pleat came to Spurs as manager he used a different line-up with Clive Allen a sole striker, but most importantly he coupled Richard Gough and Gary Mabbutt in the centre of the defence, this being a fine move. While Allen had a vintage season so did Mabbutt, putting together industry and dedication, and playing a large part in a season which promised much. Going for the grand slam, Spurs ended up in third spot in the League, losing the Football League Cup semi-final to London rivals Arsenal in a tie that went to a third-match decider. They did, however, reach the FA Cup final, but lost to Coventry City, in the match which saw Mabbutt score at both ends, netting Spurs' second goal but deflecting a Coventry cross into his own net. This he erased from the mind when, in 1991, he worried a Nottingham Forest defender into heading into his own net to give Tottenham the FA Cup. Gary also was a UEFA Cup winner with Spurs in 1984.

When Mabbutt's contract ran out in 1987 there were strong rumours that he was going to Madrid in Spain, Lyon in France, Arsenal or Manchester United. After Liverpool became the main rival for his services, he remained at White Hart Lane, saying he had been happy at Tottenham for his five seasons there, and wanted to continue his career with Spurs. He was handed the captaincy of the club and once again led by example, always playing the game fair. Owing to his style of play, Gary sustained several injuries, including a broken leg and some cuts to the head, the worse being a cheek and eye socket broken, but he always came back stronger than ever. He should have been in the England side more than he was, his sixteen matches being well spread apart. When Gary called it a day in 1998, he had made 796 appearances and scored 38 goals in his sixteen years at White Hart Lane, and was awarded the MBE in 1994. He leaves a memory of his happy smiling face as he held up the FA Cup in 1991.

Dave Mackay
Wing half 1958-1968

	Appearances	Goals
League	268	42
FA Cup	33	4
Europe	17	5
Other	44 (2)	12
TOTAL	364	

Tough tackling and always giving his best: just two of the phrases which were applied to Dave Mackay, the player whom manager Bill Nicholson once referred to as one of his best signings. Born at Musselburgh in Scotland on 13 November 1934, he was certainly one of the all-time greats of Tottenham Hotspur. Mackay showed his ability at an early age and was soon playing for Edinburgh and Scotland Schoolboys, and he was shining for minor sides Slateford Athletic and Newtongrange Star when Heart of Midlothian signed him as a part-time professional in April 1952. He was then doing his National Service but he was part of the Hearts team that took the Scottish League Cup in 1954, the Scottish Cup the next year, then went on to the Scottish League Championship in 1957/58.

It was in March 1959 that Tottenham paid out £30,000 to bring him to White Hart Lane, where he quickly made his debut versus Manchester City on 21 March 1959. He had been handed his first Scotland cap against Spain in May 1957 and was voted Scotland Player of the Year. Dave was the type of midfield performer who could win the ball for the more delicate players, such as fellow Scot John White, but this was not to say he hadn't many skills of his own, which he demonstrated in training and matches. He missed only four games in his first full season at White Hart Lane, and just five in the 'double' year. Another weapon was his long throw-in, and he scored many goals as he surged upfield, including a hat-trick against West Ham in 1962.

In December 1963 he had the misfortune to break his leg playing against Manchester United, and then suffered the same fate in a comeback game versus Shrewsbury reserves. He recovered to become Spurs captain, leading them to the FA Cup win of 1967, before he moved to Derby County in 1968, and helped them to the Second Division championship. Mackay moved into management with Swindon, Nottingham Forest, Derby County and Walsall, and then had a period in Dubai. He came home again and took charge at Doncaster and Birmingham City. Dave scored 63 goals in 364 appearances for Tottenham.

Tony Marchi
Half-back 1949-1957, 1959-1965

	Appearances	Goals
League	232	7
FA Cup	16	0
Europe	12	0
Other	57	3
TOTAL	317	

When Ron Burgess left Tottenham it was thought that no one would be able to take his place, but along came young Tony Marchi, London-born of an Italian father. He had been the understudy to Ron in Spurs two great seasons winning the Second Division and First Division consecutively. Six feet tall, Marchi was born at Edmonton on 21 January 1933, and after starring in his school teams of Edmonton, Enfield, London and Middlesex, he signed as an amateur for Tottenham in July 1948, and was playing for Spurs' reserves when just fifteen. He went on to make his senior debut for Tottenham as a seventeen-year-old on 22 April 1950 against Grimsby Town.

He gradually developed into a strong wing half with good all-round vision and was an ever-present in the 1954/55 and 1955/56 seasons. He was then given the captaincy of the club, a role in which he thrived, being a Spurs man through and through. Then along came Italian club Lanerossi with a £42,000 offer that was too good to turn down by club or player and he reluctantly moved to Italy, his father's home country. After two seasons, in which he was deemed good enough to play for Italy – this was

not to be as he had already played for England 'B' – he decided to return to England. Arsenal were very keen to sign him but his loyalty saw him return to White Hart Lane in 1959, and to a role of understudying once again, he was once dubbed the finest reserve in the country.

The famous 'double' side were being gathered at Tottenham and, although not a regular in the side, Tony more than played his part when he came into the XI; whichever player he was in for was not often missed. While the 1960/61 Spurs side picked their own XI each week, Marchi made six appearances, five for MacKay and once at centre half for Norman. The next season saw Marchi play in 21 matches, including the European Cup-Winners' Cup final, in which Spurs beat Atletico Madrid 5-1, after he had played in four other cup matches. In June 1965 Marchi left Spurs to be player-manager at Cambridge City for two years, and then the same at Northampton. His Spurs appearances were 317, with 10 goals.

Les Medley
Winger 1938-1953

	Appearances	Goals
League	150	45
FA Cup	14	1
Wartime	60	19
Other	30	9
TOTAL	254	

Born in Edmonton, on 3 September 1920, Les Medley was part of the 1951 and 1952 Tottenham side, who swept all before them in those two fine seasons. He followed other local boys playing for Edmonton, London and Middlesex Schools and signed for Tottenham as an amateur in 1935 aged fifteen, appearing for Spurs Juniors and then England Schoolboys. Just as he was turning professional in 1939 the Second World War intervened, but at first he played regularly for Spurs as well as making guest appearances for Aldershot, Orient, Millwall and West Ham.

Les was in the RAF and found himself posted to Canada, where he spent most of his time during the war, also finding himself a wife, returning to home shores in the latter war years. His Canadian wife, however, became homesick and they returned to her country in 1946, with Les playing for Toronto Greenbacks and Ulster United. But in 1948 Medley once

again came back to White Hart Lane just in time to reclaim a place in the successful Tottenham Hotspur side of the early 1950s and became an important team member of the 'push and run' side of manager Arthur Rowe.

For four seasons Les was an automatic choice in the Spurs line-up. He was programmed to appear at outside left but often roamed into other places, causing fans to shout out their own instructions if his wanderings came to nought. He was Tottenham's leading goalscorer in 1949/50 with 19 goals as they won the Second Division, playing in every game, and weighed in with 11 more in the First Division Championship side in 1951. Medley first played for England in November 1950 versus Wales. The pairing of him with Baily led to Medley playing for England six times, four of them with his Spurs partner, and not once on the losing side.

His last representative appearance was for the Rest of United Kingdom against Wales in December 1951. Once more he and his wife became unsettled and they emigrated to Canada. This time he made his life there and, although he had retired from football, he had a period as player-coach with a South African club, Randfontein, from 1958 to 1961. His last game in the famous white shirt of Tottenham was against Wolverhampton Wanderers on 25 April 1953, after scoring 74 goals in 254 appearances.

Terry Medwin
Winger 1956-1963

	Appearances	Goals
League	197	65
FA Cup	13	7
Europe	5	0
Other	32	18
TOTAL	247	

Born in Swansea on 25 September 1932, Medwin followed other players from Wales to North London. He attended St Helens School and Oxford School before he was noticed by Swansea Schools officials, and then went on to represent Wales Schools. His home team Swansea Town soon snapped up Medwin in 1946, and he turned professional in November 1949. He proved a versatile player, occupying all forward positions at Swansea. His first cap for Wales came in April 1953 as a twenty-one-year-old against Northern Ireland, and he made three appearances quite quickly, but he had been discarded by the selectors when Tottenham Hotspur signed him for £18,000 in April 1956.

His form on the Spurs right wing soon saw him back in the Wales XI, and he ended with 29 caps for his country. In his first season at White Hart Lane Terry helped Spurs to runners-up position in the First Division, scoring 14 goals in the process. He was a regular amongst the goals during his Tottenham career, and his top performance was four goals in the 6-0 victory over Leicester City on 7 March 1959, but this was only Spurs' ninth win in a poor season when they slumped to eighteenth spot in the First Division. This came in a spell in which they were never lower than third in a period of six years from 1956 to 1963. Medwin was not a regular in the great Spurs 'double' side but played in just enough matches to gain a championship medal, being understudy for both wing positions. He was restored to the outside right spot in the next season, which ended with him gaining an FA Cup winners' medal. A fast and direct winger, he was always amongst the goals, popping up with several match-winners.

Medwin spent ten happy years at Tottenham before suffering a broken leg in a match against NSAFL when on tour to South Africa in May 1963, but he gave up after failing to regain full fitness. He became manager of Enfield, followed by the same post at Cheshunt, then returned to Wales as a coach at Cardiff City. Spells then came with Norwich City and back at Swansea as coach and then scout. His 247 appearances for Spurs saw him notch 90 goals.

	Appearances	Goals
League	248	95
S. League	9	4
FA Cup	19	6
Wartime	15	14
Other	52	36
TOTAL	343	

For many years Billy Minter was associated with Tottenham Hotspur as a player, manager and trainer. He was born in Woolwich, south London on 16 April 1888 and started his career with two games as an amateur at Norwich City in November 1905. He then returned to his birthplace and assisted Woolwich Arsenal but failed to create an impression and, after a two-year spell at Reading, where he was their top scorer both times, he signed for Tottenham in March 1908.

Minter was put straight into the first team where he scored his first goal for Spurs against Millwall, although Spurs lost 2-1. He went on to be the regular inside right for ten years and a more dependable player you could not wish for, helping Tottenham to promotion to the First Division in their first season in the Football

League. Minter was quite well built and, as a result, was hard to push off the ball. He was a regular goalscorer for the club, topping the Spurs' list in his first three years at White Hart Lane. He became captain of the Spurs when Daniel Steele retired in 1912, and when his legs became a mite weary for regular first-team football, he took over as trainer of the Tottenham club. He was then absent during the First World War and only managed to play for Spurs at odd times, but it was Minter who was the trainer when they won the FA Cup in 1921.

He had apparently played his last match for Tottenham at Hull City on 26 December 1919, but went on to appear in two friendlies when the team was short: at West Ham United in February 1924 and at Hull City in March 1926. When manager Peter McWilliam left for Middlesbrough, Billy Minter became team manager for almost three years, but in his first full season Tottenham were relegated, and when he failed to get them back up again, suffering from ill health, he resigned in November 1929. Spurs were so keen not to lose such a good servant of the club that he was not allowed to leave and he became assistant secretary, a post he held right up to the time of his death on 21 May 1940. He had been living in Bruce Grove Road. As a director said, he was 'a real loveable gentleman.' Billy Minter scored 155 goals in his 343 appearances for Tottenham Hotspur.

Tom Morris
Half-back 1899-1913

	Appearances	Goals
League	63	2
S. League	239	21
W. League	80	11
FA Cup	39	1
Wartime	30	4
Other	72	9
TOTAL	523	

Although born in Grantham, Lincolnshire, on 9 February 1875, Tom Morris was virtually a one-club man, spending thirteen years at White Hart Lane. He made his Southern League debut for Tottenham at home to Queens Park Rangers on 9 September 1899, playing his part in a win by the only goal in front of an 11,000 crowd. He was also in the Spurs line-up for their first match in the Football League on 1 September 1908, scoring one of the goals in the 3-0 win over Wolverhampton Wanderers. Morris had started his football career with Grantham Rovers and Gainsborough Trinity, where he played at centre half, but on his move to north London he became a fixture in the right half position for Tottenham in their Southern League days. They won the championship in the season 1899/1900, Tom Morris weighing in with six goals.

In 1901 came a feat which will never be repeated, when Tottenham Hotspur, as a non-League club, won the FA Cup by beating the mighty Sheffield United 3-1 in a replay at Burnden Park, Bolton; the first match at Crystal Palace had been drawn 2-2. During this vintage Spurs season, Morris also figured at inside right as well as in his proper position at wing half, and one game at centre half. He was a key member of this side and a powerful influence in the Southern League days for Spurs, whom he had joined in preference to other top clubs who saw his potential. He never seemed to tire and was always in the centre of the action in all his games, although some regarded him as 'a little rough'. He appeared in more Southern League matches than any other Tottenham player.

Although he played in two international trial matches, North *v.* South, in 1900 and 1903, Morris was not favoured by the England selectors and missed out on the England career which he rightfully deserved. After thirteen eventful years at White Hart Lane, during which time he was given two benefit matches, Morris played his last competitive game for Spurs in a London FA Charity Cup encounter with Crystal Palace on 28 October 1912, at the age of thirty-seven. He remained at Tottenham, however, and was a long-serving member of the ground staff up to his death in April 1942. He scored 48 goals in his 523 appearances for Spurs.

John Morrison
Centre forward 1932-1946

	Appearances	Goals
League	134	90
FA Cup	21	14
Wartime	33	25
Other	2	3
TOTAL	190	

Born in Belvedere, in Kent, on 26 March 1911, John Morrison was a unique goalscorer at Tottenham, remembered for often missing the easiest of scoring chances but netting the ball from some impossible positions, and for goals knocked in via his back and other parts of his body. There was no denying he also possessed better than average skills. He joined Spurs from his first club Callenders Athletic, initially as an amateur in August 1931, and was loaned out to nursery club Northfleet eight months later, where his frequent scoring was noticed.

Turning professional in July 1933, Morrison made his Tottenham debut at Chesterfield on 1 April 1933, scoring the Spurs' only goal in a 1-1 draw. However this proved to be his only outing during that season. He failed to make it into the seniors at all in the 1933/34 season, although he had notched 36 goals in 28 matches for the reserves. George Hunt was the preferred centre forward at that time. Morrison came into the First XI the next season, although it was only in a handful of matches that he and Hunt were in the side together.

John was the one to top the list with 28 goals as they shared positions in the next campaign. Hunt then moved from Tottenham, leaving Morrison to lead the Spurs forwards in a goalscoring spree in 1934/35. He registered a hat-trick at West Bromwich Albion in a match that was wiped from the records at the beginning of the 1939/40 season as war broke out. Morrison was unable to play at White Hart Lane for a short spell, as he was working in the Royal Arsenal at Woolwich, but was back at centre forward very soon.

Towards the end of the first war season he netted hat-tricks in 4 out of 5 games versus Charlton Athletic, Brentford, Portsmouth and Southampton quite a feat at the best of times but he didn't feature for Spurs during the rest of the war. He tried a comeback on 29 December 1945 at Leicester City and, after a 4-0 defeat, Morrison decided he was not the player he used to be and retired. In 190 appearances for Tottenham he scored 132 goals, a very good average which would possibly have been greater if the war had not intervened.

Alan Mullery MBE
Half-back 1963-1972

	Appearances	Goals
League	313	25
FA Cup	33	1
League Cup	18	0
Europe	10	4
Other	55	10
TOTAL	429	

A servant for nearly ten years for Tottenham Hotspur, Alan was born in Notting Hill in West London on 23 November 1941. He would agree he did not have the skills of Stanley Matthews, but he gave his best in every game he played in for Spurs, Fulham and for England. After playing for London and Middlesex Schools, Mullery joined the Fulham ground staff in June 1957, upgrading to the professional ranks the next year. Within two months of signing for Fulham, he made his debut at seventeen years of age, and kept his newly won place in the cottagers line-up. After over 200 appearances for Fulham, and winning his first England Under-23 cap in November 1960, Alan moved across London to join Tottenham for £72,500 in March 1964. He had been acquired by Spurs to take over the mantle of Danny Blanchflower, who had retired in the early part of the 1963/64 season, and for part of his early Tottenham career he was weighed up against the Spurs legend; and the fans were slow to accept his place in the team, as he was a different sort of player to Blanchflower. He couldn't have had a harder debut for Spurs, this being against Manchester United on 21 March 1964, but after he settled down to play in his own style, which was more steady than exciting, the Spurs fans soon accepted him. He was one of the best wing halves around at the time and soon gained an England place in December 1964. He went on to play for his country on 35 occasions, and was captain in some matches. He also took over as Tottenham captain when Dave Mackay moved to Derby County in 1968, and led Spurs to victory in the League Cup against Aston Villa in 1971. He was loaned back to his first club, Fulham, in 1971, returning to Spurs for their UEFA Cup win in 1972. His final permanent move back to Fulham in 1972, for £65,000, saw him play almost another 200 times for them. He had appeared 429 times for Spurs, scoring 40 goals, and received an MBE for his services to football. He was also voted Player of the Year in 1975. On retiring he went on to manage Brighton & Hove Albion, Charlton Athletic, Crystal Palace, Queens Park Rangers, and then Brighton again in 1986.

Jimmy Neighbour
Winger 1970-1977

	Appearances	Goals
League	104 (15)	8
FA Cup	10 (1)	1
League Cup	14 (3)	1
Europe	6 (3)	1
Other	24 (10)	4
TOTAL	190	

In the 1970s, Jimmy Neighbour was an old fashioned winger, which was not so bad, as Spurs took him to their heart, like they do all players with a high degree of skill. He was born in Chingford, Essex, on 15 November 1950, attending Whitehall County School and was captain of his next school, Heathcote, where a sports master commented, 'Right from the first moment he stood out, and I knew he would make it to the top.' His first organised football came with Waltham Forest Schools; he then progressed via both London and Essex Schools, joining Spurs as an apprentice in April 1966 and turning professional just over two years later. Jimmy made his debut at Stoke City as a substitute on 24 October 1970, and made quite an impression on a corner post when he accidentally broke it in half when taking a corner kick. He had been given his chance when Roger Morgan was injured but then traded starts with Jimmy Pearce for a while. Neighbour made six more appearances as a sub and started the game on 19 other occasions, all in his first season,

which was crowned by playing in Tottenham's successful League Cup win over Aston Villa 2-0, at the age of twenty. Jimmy's great skill was the best part of his game, twisting and turning, although he could easily be knocked off the ball by more robust defenders. He also displayed his versatility by playing on both wings and liked to take the ball right to the goal-line, sending across some tantalising balls. It was when Terry Neill took over as manager that Neighbour was an automatic choice, his best season being 1975/76, when he played in 44 out of 51 Spurs games. When Neill departed, Jimmy found himself in and out of the side once more, as Taylor and Coates were brought to White Hart Lane. Many supporters were dismayed when he was let go to Norwich City for £75,000, just after his last match for Tottenham against the Canaries on 25 September 1976. Spurs were relegated at the end of that season. Jimmy spent three years in Norfolk, followed by four more at West Ham, and then he retired. He turned to coaching, especially the youth sides, making a return to White Hart Lane in the twenty-first century in this capacity. In his Tottenham career Neighbour scored 15 goals in 190 appearances, being more of a supplier then a marksman.

	Appearances	Goals
League	124	0
FA Cup	5	0
Other	10	0
TOTAL	139	

For almost ten years Nicholls performed as one of the best of goalkeepers at White Hart Lane. His 6ft 4in build could look much larger when an opposing forward was bearing down on the Tottenham Hotspur goal. He was born in Canton, Nottinghamshire, on 8 March 1905 and, as befits a man of his height, he joined the army and entered the Grenadier Guards. It was when he was playing for the Grenadier Guards that Spurs took notice and, with a scout watching him, Joe put on a spectacular display in the Army Services Bulldog Challenge Cup final. They kept a constant watch over the big man, and when they learnt that he had decided to leave the army they quickly asked him to sign for Spurs. Other clubs had been doing the same thing, watching and waiting, but Tottenham beat them all when he accepted their offer to join the White Hart Lane outfit.

Spurs then sent him off to their nursery club, Northfleet in Kent, to develop and further his goalkeeping skills. One of his special skills was his ability to throw the ball very long distances, which usually brought a gasp of astonishment from those seeing this for the first time. He made his debut for Tottenham at Liverpool on 30 April 1927, and this was his only appearance that year. He played only a few games over the next four years, and did not feature at all in one season. He became more or less a regular in the 1932/33 promotion season, and an ever-present the following year. Nicholls was also a brave goalkeeper, as seen from a match against Fulham in December 1932, which was drawn 2-2. A penalty for Fulham saw their centre forward hit the ball so hard and true that it bounced back off Nicholls nearly to the halfway line, and Nicholls collapsed on the spot. When he was revived he went on to play the game of his life, as Spurs were promoted that year.

The closest he came to international fame was a match for The Rest v. England in 1934. His last match was on 13 April 1936 against Charlton Athletic. When Nicholls was allowed to leave in 1936, he joined Bristol Rovers after 139 appearances for Spurs.

Bill Nicholson OBE

Wing half 1938-1955

	Appearances	Goals
League	318	6
FA Cup	27	0
Wartime	12	0
Other	38	1
TOTAL	395	

One of the great legends of Tottenham Hotspur is Bill Nicholson, who was the architect of one of the finest club sides the world has ever seen, but before that put his heart and soul into playing, and helping his one and only club, of which he is now president. Many supporters, Spurs and otherwise, have thought for many years that he should be awarded a knighthood for all the work and effort that he has put into football, not just for Tottenham but for British sport in general. Any time he made an appearance at White Hart Lane in the present day he was revered by all, many thinking they are in the presence of greatness which of course they were. He was born on 26 January 1919 at Scarborough in Yorkshire and on leaving school he played for the local working men's club and Scarborough Liberals, until he was offered a trial with Spurs.

He joined the Tottenham ground staff in March 1936 and was at the Spurs' nursery side

Northfleet for two years before making his Spurs debut. This came on 22 October 1938, away to Blackburn Rovers in the Second Division, playing at left-back – not his proper position, but he buckled down to make a good impression. This he must have done as he had eight matches in that position before the end of the season. He also appeared in the three League matches at the start of the 1939/40 season before the War came along to change things. Just when he had broken into the senior Spurs XI, the Second World War interrupted his career, as it did for hundreds of professional footballers all over the country, and it saw Bill go back to his native Yorkshire; he then joined the Durham Light infantry. He only played four games for Spurs during the war, but found quite regular matches with Fulham, Hartlepool, Middlesbrough, Sunderland, Newcastle, Darlington and even Manchester United, as he was stationed most of the time in the north of the country.

It was halfway through the first peacetime season that Nicholson made his comeback for Tottenham, when he appeared against Fulham on 9 March 1946, and at centre half Bill staked his claim for a place in the Spurs line-up when football seriously resumed in 1945/46, moving to his preferred position at right half soon after. Never a spectacular player, Nicholson was one

Bill Nicholson received many awards during his time as manager of Tottenham Hotspur. Here he has been presented with a silver tray.

of the hard working and dour players who carried on giving 100 per cent every week, winning the ball before switching it to the more creative players in the Tottenham team. He was unlucky in having played for England just once against Portugal in May 1951, when he scored with his first kick. He was an England reserve on numerous occasions, also in the World Cup party of 1950. He also played for England 'B' and the Football League.

When he retired from playing, after 395 appearances and 7 goals, he became a coach at White Hart Lane, and also coached Cambridge University, before moving up to become manager, taking over from Jimmy Anderson in 1958. He announced his arrival as Spurs manager with an amazing 10-4 win over Everton on 11 October. Within two years Tottenham Hotspur had won the 'double' and Bill proudly watched Blanchflower collect the cup.

Nicholson led Spurs to their greatest honours: three FA Cups, two League Cups, the European Cup-Winners' Cup and the UEFA Cup quite a haul.

When pressed to tell which of the many matches that Tottenham Hotspur played he thinks was the greatest, Bill Nicholson opts for winning the European Cup-Winners' Cup by beating Atletico Madrid in Rotterdam. He also has a soft spot for the 1961 side who became the first team to complete the League and cup double in the twentieth century. He was awarded the OBE in 1975, for his immense work within the game, and the Professional Footballers Association Merit Award in 1984. He was manager until September 1974, and, until he passed away last year, he was the club president. The short road to the main entrance of White Hart Lane is now named Bill Nicholson Way.

Maurice Norman
Centre half 1955-1966

	Appearances	Goals
League	357	16
FA Cup	37	2
Europe	17	1
Other	42	0
TOTAL	453	

A giant centre half, Maurice Norman began his professional career at Norwich City before arriving at White Hart Lane to play a large part in the 'double' team. He was born in Mulbarton in Norfolk on 8 May 1934. In his mid-teens his football centred on Norfolk Schools, Wymondham Minors and Mulbarton FC, and he signed for Norwich City in September 1952. After a quiet spell at Carrow Road, Maurice was soon making his presence felt and played his first game for Norwich City in February 1955 at centre half; he had only played 35 League matches when Spurs came to call.

He moved to White Hart Lane for £28,000, with Johnny Gavin moving the other way back to Norfolk. Norman, who was brought to Spurs to take Alf Ramsey's place, was in the Tottenham team at right-back for his debut against Cardiff City on 5 November 1955. The following February he gained his first England Under-23 cap against Scotland, still at right-back.

He missed a long spell in 1956 through injury, and when he returned it was to left-back, this lasting only a handful of games before he settled in as a powerful figure at centre half. He missed only one match when Spurs won both League and FA Cup in 1961, and scored four goals, including the only Tottenham goal at Sheffield Wednesday when they lost their first game of the 'double' season.

He gained his first full England cap against Peru in May 1962, and was England's regular centre half from then on, winning 22 more caps. Already an uncompromising tackler, he began to lay off many skilful passes as his game improved. Norman was also very useful when corners or free-kicks were on offer, many of his goals coming from set pieces. Being tall, he did not always rely on his hard tackles as he developed as more of an interceptor of the ball, his long legs often stretching out to claim the ball when an opposing attacker thought they had got away from his grip. Come 1965, and once more at right-back, Norman received a very badly broken leg in a friendly against a Hungary XI; this resulted in the end of his playing career after eleven seasons at White Hart Lane. He had scored 19 goals in 453 appearances for Tottenham.

Eugene 'Taffy' O'Callaghan
Inside forward 1926-1935, 1940-1944

	Appearances	Goals
League	252	92
FA Cup	11	6
Wartime	20	4
Other	30	19
TOTAL	313	

Born in Ebbw Vale on 6 October 1906, O'Callaghan was a real artist in football. He had played for Wales Schools, but on leaving school went straight into working in the coal pits of South Wales, and it wasn't until he was nineteen that he was noticed by a scout when turning out for Ebbw Vale reserves. It was in 1925 that young Taffy O'Callaghan arrived at White Hart Lane and at first the manager thought him too small, but he impressed in trial matches. Taffy took his chance when Tottenham favourite Jimmy Seed was injured and he found himself a young lad in the company of older and more experienced players. He made his debut at Everton on 15 February 1927 and by the end of that season was becoming quite a regular in the side, equally at home in both inside forward positions. As an artist uses paint, O'Callaghan used the ball and he cost the club just a small signing on fee.

Taffy was an ever-present in the next season and topped the goalscoring chart for Spurs with 28 goals, including four in one match against Everton at White Hart Lane. O'Callaghan was always hungry for the ball and full of enthusiasm, and was known in his early days as a 'boy wonder'; he always tried hard to live up to that description. He was also a shining light in the poor Tottenham sides in the late 1920s, and in their yo-yo years that followed. O'Callaghan helped Tottenham to win promotion in 1933 and was also in the side a year later when they went straight down again.

Usually a clever ball-player is not a prolific goalscorer, but Taffy was different as he matched his skills with a hard shot in either foot for such a small frame, and scored goals regularly. He made his first appearance for Wales against Northern Ireland in May 1929 and was awarded ten more caps while with Spurs. Surprisingly he moved to Leicester City in 1935, then Fulham two years later. Although he was a Fulham player, he returned to White Hart Lane when nearly forty years of age to play for Tottenham during the war years. Taffy narrowly missed out on a century of League goals for Tottenham, his total being 92; in his 313 full total appearances he produced 121 goals.

Frank Osborne

Centre forward 1923-1931

	Appearances	Goals
League	210	78
FA Cup	9	4
Other	9	5
TOTAL	228	

Although Osborne played twice for England while with Tottenham Hotspur, he was born in Wynberg in South Africa, on 14 October 1896. His father was a colonel in the Army Medical Corps and Frank was fifteen when his family returned to England in 1911. Residing in south-east London, he played for top amateur side Bromley from 1919 and made a late start to his professional career when he signed for Fulham after two seasons as an amateur in Kent. At Fulham for just over two seasons, Osborne made 70 League and FA Cup appearances while he gained two caps for England: at centre forward against Ireland and on the right wing against France.

He was not a well built forward but he made up for this with a great positional sense and he knew exactly when and how to lay the ball off to his fellow forwards. With Jimmy Cantrell beginning to show his age, Tottenham were on the look out for a replacement, and they laid out £1,500 to bring Osborne to White Hart Lane in January 1924. He made his debut almost immediately at home to Newcastle United and

was soon reckoned to be more or less a regular in the side, but for a player brought in to score goals, his first six months provided only one. However he was not at centre forward at first, filling both inside forward positions and even having a full season as the outside right, finding the net just twice. It was in 1925/26 that he showed his worth as leader of the forward line and top-scored with 27, missing only five games. From then he still moved about the forward line and to his credit he gave of his best wherever he was played. He gained two more England caps while with Spurs; the second one versus Belgium saw him grab a hat-trick at centre forward.

His career was coming to a close when he moved to Southampton for £450; he finshed after two years playing on the south coast after two years and joined the board of directors' back at Fulham. He moved into management at Craven Cottage, guiding Fulham to promotion in his first year, then filling other managerial positions before finally putting his feet up. Despite his moving around positions he scored 87 goals in his 228 appearances at Tottenham Hotspur.

Jimmy Pearce
Forward 1968-1975

	Appearances	Goals
League	109 (33)	21
FA Cup	4 (6)	3
League Cup	21 (6)	7
Europe	8 (7)	4
Other	18 (7)	8
TOTAL	219	

Local lad makes good could have been the story of Jimmy Pearce's time with Tottenham Hotspur. He was born in Tottenham on 27 November 1947 and became associated with the Spurs while still at school, and as with some others who came up through the ranks from local football he didn't find it so easy. He was selected for Tottenham Boys XI when only fifteen, and joined the professional ranks at White Hart Lane in May 1965. While playing for Tottenham Schools he also appeared with England Schoolboys. Jimmy could well have been in another sport, his father Jim, a PT Instructor in the Army, was supporting him as a young boxer when still at school. He even won the district title for his weight on two occasions, but football won as Jimmy thought he could make it in that sport. Being small as a youngster he soon adopted a dogged attitude, but was not averse to darting runs at the opponent's defence. While Pearce could play in all forward positions, his favourite was as a striker, or centre forward as they called it then, but he played some of his best football as a winger.

He made his senior Spurs debut on their 1968 summer tour of Greece and Cyprus, and his first League appearance came at the beginning of the following season, in a local derby on 10 August against Arsenal. Although not a regular, Jimmy played 31 games that season. Although he missed out through injury in the 1971 Football League Cup win versus Aston Villa, he was a part of the 1973 League Cup winning team that defeated Norwich City in the final. Periods in the starting line-up were also shared with many matches on the substitute bench, but Jimmy was always scoring goals whenever needed. Many Spurs supporters probably thought Jimmy was capable of more, but he was always a favourite with the crowd.

At twenty-six, however, came a body blow as a knee injury was diagnosed as being a rare bone complaint, and in 1974 he was forced into early retirement. After a year's rest, Pearce attempted a comeback with non-League Walthamstow Avenue, but to no avail. His last game for Spurs was on 3 August 1974 in a friendly at Hearts in Scotland. His playing days ended and his 219 appearances produced 43 goals.

	Appearances	Goals
League	654 (2)	31
FA Cup	69	2
League Cup	66	3
Europe	63 (1)	3
Other	162 (5)	13
TOTAL	1,022	

With over 1,000 appearances for Tottenham Hotspur, Steve Perryman was a king amongst one-club men, being on the White Hart Lane stage for seventeen years from 1969 to 1986. He was born in Ealing, in west London, on 21 December 1951, at a time when the Spurs were sweeping all before them in the Second Division and again driving on to the First Division Championship. It must have been fate that Perryman joined Tottenham and led them to many triumphs during his long career at White Hart Lane. His time at the club saw them go through the ups of the early 1970s, then suffer relegation for one season, before returning to win more trophies in the 1980s.

Steve came to prominence playing for Ealing Schoolboys, London Boys and then the England Schools, before Tottenham snapped him up as an apprentice in July 1967. He was then upgraded to the full professional ranks in January 1969 and he went with the Spurs party, at the end of the 1968/69 season, on their tour of North America. He made his first appearance for a Spurs team versus the touring West Ham United at Baltimore on 15 May 1969, and played in all four matches on the tour. Making his Football League debut on 27 September 1969, Steve played 24 games in the League and four FA Cup matches by the end of his first full season; he also scored his first Tottenham goal against Crystal Palace on Boxing Day 1969.

He showed his versatility by wearing four different numbers on his shirt in his first full season, but was basically a bustling midfielder throughout his long Spurs career. Sometimes at his best going forward, he scored many an important goal for Tottenham. He was in the unique position, when the Tottenham youth team won the FA Youth Cup in 1970, of already being a regular first-team player. Throughout his years at White Hart Lane, Perryman shone as a superior all-round footballer, with strength coupled with honesty, and maturity beyond his years. From his first game onwards he was undoubtedly the first name pencilled in on the team sheet each week by all four managers he served under at White Hart Lane.

Out of the 58 Spurs games in 1970/71 Steve missed only two, as they went on to win the Football League Cup and finish third in the League. He also had a spell when he missed just one game out of 342. His first international recognition came with the England Under-23 team versus East Germany in 1972, going on to play 17 times, but won only a solitary full cap

Steve Perryman is seen here in the Spurs' colours when they had one season in the Second Division. With him as captain, they came straight back to the top flight.

for England, against Iceland. He certainly should have played more matches for England, but he played in so many positions in the Tottenham XI for the good of his club, this was always seen as the reason he was overlooked.

When Martin Peters left for Norwich City, in March 1975, Perryman was made captain of Spurs, a role he revelled in for eleven years, and although they dropped into the Second Division, under Perryman's hard driving they returned to where they belonged after one season in the basement. Only once in his stay at White Hart Lane did he have a poor spell when even his goals, which were never in plenty, dried up. Steve buckled down to turn this around, doing so with a return to his better self in the home leg of the UEFA Cup in 1972. The cheers echoed around White Hart Lane on 5 April when Spurs faced

Italian giants AC Milan, and Pennyman drove in two beautifully volleyed edge-of-the-box goals. In his own unspectacular words, 'after putting on the pressure they broke away and went a goal up, and they were supposed to be the masters of the clean sheet, and it seemed our goals were to come from outside the penalty area.' In his time as captain, Tottenham had two FA Cup wins, two UEFA Cup victories and three other finals, and Steve gained the honour of an MBE in 1986.

He left Spurs in March 1986 for Oxford and a year later came back to London as player, then manager, at Brentford. Steve had a spell at Tottenham as assistant to Ossie Ardiles in the Argentine player's short reign. He scored 52 goals in his record 1,022 appearances for Spurs.

	Appearances	Goals
League	189	46
FA Cup	16	5
League Cup	23	12
Europe	32	13
Other	27	11
TOTAL	287	

Although best known for his exploits in the England World Cup success of 1966, and dubbed 'ten years ahead of his time' by Alf Ramsey, Martin Peters came to White Hart Lane for £200,000 in March 1970. This sum was the record laid out for a player at the time. Part of the deal was Jimmy Greaves moving to West Ham United, where he retired after just one year, while Peters had a fruitful five years at White Hart Lane. Born in Plaistow, in east London, he progressed from his local Dagenham Schools, through Essex Schools to London and England Boys, arriving at West Ham United as a professional in November 1960.

Martin's ten years at West Ham are fully documented elsewhere and if another club would benefit from this classy player it was to be Tottenham Hotspur; when he arrived he quickly fitted into the Spurs way of playing. Already the holder of 33 caps for England, he was still only twenty-six and probably at his peak. Peters celebrated his first match in a Spurs shirt with a headed goal against Coventry City on 21 March 1970. For a midfield player he grabbed more than his share of goals, his knack of drifting in behind the defence was really a trademark, and although every defender was aware of this move, it brought Spurs a goal on many occasions. Being a classy footballer, some questioned his work rate, as supporters do with those players of ability, but Martin could go through the toughest of games shrugging off the hardest tackles and getting on with his job.

When Alan Mullery left Tottenham, Peters was the obvious choice for the post of captain in 1972. Another 34 international appearances in his time at White Hart Lane increased his total England caps, and he was a member of the side that won the League Cup in 1971 and 1973 and the UEFA Cup in 1972. When Terry Neill arrived at Spurs as manager, a disagreement led to Peters leaving after five years of fine service for Spurs, and he was transferred to Norwich City for £60,000. He spent another five years with the Norfolk club before becoming player-coach, and then manager, for Sheffield United, retiring in 1981, although he then had a spell with Gorleston Town. He arrived back at Tottenham as a director of the club in the late 1990s. Martin was awarded the MBE in 1978. His appearances for Spurs were 287 and his goals tallied 87.

John Pratt
Midfield 1969-1986

	Appearances	Goals
League	307 (24)	39
FA Cup	23 (5)	2
League Cup	27 (4)	7
Europe	24 (1)	1
Other	81 (12)	16
TOTAL	508	

Born in Hackney on 26 June 1948, John was a Londoner through and through and, apart from a three-year spell with Portland Timbers in the United States, he played the majority of his football in London. John had played at youth level for London and had joined Brentford for a year before former Spurs star Terry Medwin recommended him to Tottenham, and he went to White Hart Lane in November 1965. He had been a centre half when at school and youth level, but being only 5ft 8in he decided to move to wing half. Working his way through the 'A' side and the reserves, John made his League debut against Arsenal at Highbury on 24 March 1969, although he had appeared against a Cyprus XI on the Spurs summer tour of 1968. A utility player in every sense of the word, John seemed to settle into the right half position after Alan Mullery moved back to Fulham, and virtually made the no.4 shirt his own in the early 1970s. He was a non-stop, all-action type of player and a ball-winner who let the more skilful members of the team ply their trade, but he was a team member that Tottenham always relied on when the going got tough. He suffered a disappointment when an injury forced him to retire from Spurs' successful League Cup victory of 1973, limping off as early as the twentieth minute, then seeing his replacement Coates net the winning goal. Going down to the Second Division in 1977, John was an ever-present the following season, which saw Tottenham climb straight back up. Never one to acclaim as a prolific goalscorer, the goals he scored were of vital importance and often of the spectacular sort which goalkeepers could only stand and watch. For some strange reason a small section of the White Hart Lane crowd seemed to take a dislike to the midfield dynamo, but he showed how much he meant to most supporters when over 24,000 attended his testimonial game with Arsenal in 1978. He remained with Tottenham until 1980, when he went to play in America, but returned to Spurs first as a youth coach and assistant manager to Peter Shreeves. He kept playing in the ex-Spurs team, playing for charity. Pratt scored 65 goals in 508 appearances.

Full-back 1949-1955

	Appearances	Goals
League	226	24
FA Cup	24	0
Other	33	6
TOTAL	283	

Alf Ramsey was born in Dagenham in 1922, the son of a smallholder, and had ambitions to be nothing more than a grocer. His three older brothers, however, taught him to play football, not knowing they were doing a great service for British and world football. At the age of seven he made it into the junior team at Beacontree Heath School, playing at inside left while brother Len was at inside right. By the time Alf reached nine he was centre half and captain of the school XI. Next step up was Dagenham Schools, the first game being against West Ham, and then a place in the Essex Schools XI. A spell as an apprentice at the Co-operative stores followed, which meant working all day on Saturdays; Alf played for a local side, Five Elms, on Thursday afternoons. A scout from Portsmouth first noticed him, but after signing amateur forms for them, he was not contacted again.

The Second World War came along and he was called up in 1940 and posted to Cornwall to learn how to be a soldier. Alf took a major step up in the soccer world, soon representing his battalion, where he was a Sergeant in the AA based in Hampshire, and in 1943 he figured at centre half in a match against Southampton who won 10-1. The Saints were impressed, however, and he was asked to play at Luton where, although they won 3-2, Alf gave away a penalty. Still an amateur, he was paid just his expenses, a twopenny halfpenny tram fare. Turning professional in 1946, he made his debut in a match against Arsenal, who were playing their war games at White Hart Lane, and the following week he returned to meet Tottenham Hotspur on the same ground. It was in a match against Barnsley that he scored from the penalty spot for the first time. Now a regular in the Southampton side, he was selected first for England 'B' v. Switzerland, followed by representing the Football League v. Irish League, and made his full debut in December 1948 against Switzerland.

At the age of twenty-nine he moved to Tottenham Hotspur for £21,000, with Ernie Jones moving in the opposite direction. Alf played his first game as a Spurs player for England against Italy at White Hart Lane, and kept his international place for the next 28 England matches, being captain whenever Billy Wright was absent. Alf was a stylish and precision-like defender, and a regular in man-

Alf Ramsey clears the ball for England v. Italy at White Hart Lane.

ager Arthur Rowe's great side which won the Second Division and First Division, in 1950 and 1951 respectively. He was the side's, and England's, penalty kick expert. Alf built up a great understanding with Ted Ditchburn, and many a Tottenham attack started from these two men. A favourite ploy was to use the back pass to the goalkeeper, but this broke down when, in the FA Cup semi-final against Blackpool in 1953 at Villa Park, Mudie nipped in to score the winning goal.

When Ron Burgess left Spurs, Ramsey was his natural successor as captain, before he retired. It was a minor surprise when he was appointed manager of Ipswich Town, who were then in the Third Division (South) in August 1955. Alf had no real qualifications but in his first full season he took them to the Third Division Championship. Players had a lot of respect for him, and more success was to come when he led Ipswich to promotion to the First Division

for the first time ever, following this by taking the First Division title. He had shaped a team of mostly unknowns into an impressive football machine.

The FA were the next to recognise Ramsey's worth and appointed him manager of England in 1963; he responded by instantly doing away with the selection committee, and taking full charge. He then made his well-known statement saying that England would win the World Cup in 1966, when it was played in England. He delivered as he promised, the World Cup being won at Wembley in 1966, with a 4-2 victory over West Germany. He remained England manager until May 1974, when he was dismissed as England failed to qualify for the World Cup that year, but he was certainly the most successful of England managers. After a short spell as caretaker manager at Birmingham City, he retired, having been knighted in 1966, and settled into his home at Ipswich, where he had lived for many years.

Outside left 1951-1959

	Appearances	Goals
League	182	53
FA Cup	18	5
Other	24	7
TOTAL	224	

George Robb was an amateur player for a great deal of his career with Finchley, where he won eighteen England Amateur caps in the nine years spent at the club. Born in Finsbury Park on 1 June 1926, Robb's skill was recognised at an early age when he shone for his schools in Islington and Finchley, and Tottenham were interested enough to sign him on amateur forms in 1944. In those hectic war years this was not followed up and he was not offered professional terms, so George became a schoolteacher while playing for Finchley.

When Les Medley finally quit England for life in Canada, Spurs struggled to find a replacement for quite a while and they tried several players in the outside left position, some disappearing after one match. The answer lay on their doorstep; George Robb had already made his Spurs debut on 25 December 1951 at Charlton Athletic, and scored in the 3-0 win. He had also played 6 games the following season with 3 goals. In 1953/54 George was seen as the best candidate and was persuaded to turn professional at the late age of twenty-seven.

He became virtually an ever-present on the left wing and shared top spot on the scoring chart with Walters, his right-wing colleague, each man netting 16 goals as Spurs struggled to keep above the relegation zone. Robb was not a delicate player by any means, as his predecessor had been, but his skill was his strong running and willingness to chase long balls, and to have a go from any position he found himself in. For the next four seasons he missed only a handful of matches and was such a success that he was even selected for the full England team for their game versus Hungary in November 1953. It was unfortunate that this meeting was remembered as the one that England lost heavily, and George was not picked again. He did however play in three 'B' internationals at the end of the 1853/54 season, and he was undoubtedly at his peak around this time.

In 1957 he was unfortunate to suffer a serious injury to his knee, which slowed him up considerably, and although he tried to play on the following year, the knee was too troublesome. He was forced into retirement, and a full-time career back in the classroom. George Robb scored 65 goals in his 224 appearances for Tottenham.

Graham Roberts
Defender, midfield 1979-1988

	Appearances	Goals
League	200 (9)	23
FA Cup	27	2
League Cup	24 (1)	5
Europe	25 (1)	6
Other	81 (6)	10
TOTAL	374	

Born in Southampton on 3 July 1959, Roberts came into the football spotlight quite late after his local club Southampton rejected him. He had been on their books as a schoolboy, although he had represented Southampton and Hampshire Schools. He then began to turn out for non-League Sholing before Bournemouth signed him as a youth and he again left after they abandoned their youth policy. Recovering from a broken foot, Graham had just less than three years at Dorchester Town and a spell with Weymouth, where he attracted attention from bigger clubs. In May 1980 Tottenham stepped in to bring him to White Hart Lane for £35,000, a record fee for a non-League player. He went straight into the line-up for two friendlies at the end of this season and in 1980/81, after two games as a substitute, he broke into the team and gained an FA Cup winners' medal at the end of his first season. The cash paid out proved a bargain when Graham cemented his place in the white shirt of Tottenham. He was an all-out, fearless midfielder-cum-defender who, although not a particular fast player, would nevertheless win challenges with ferocious desire, and for all this he often surprised supporters with a flash of creative ability. He also became a folk hero with the Spurs crowd, who still liked hard performers as well as those who had the finer skills, and it was one of his bursts from midfield that led to the match-winning penalty against Queens Park Rangers in Spurs' FA Cup victory of 1982. It was from midfield that Roberts scored a hat-trick against his home town Southampton in March 1982, and this brought him recognition as he played his first England match in May 1983 versus Northern Ireland. He went on to gain a further five caps for England while at Tottenham. Probably one of his most influential goals was in the 1984 UEFA Cup final at White Hart Lane against Anderlecht, to force a penalty shoot-out. Spurs duly won. Graham was captain that night with Perryman injured, and a picture remains of his triumphant toothy smile as he held high the trophy. With a new manager at Spurs, Roberts was allowed to move to Rangers, and two years later he returned south to Chelsea as player-coach, ending his career with spells at West Bromwich Albion and Enfield. His 374 appearances for Spurs saw him notch 46 goals.

Jimmy Robertson

Winger 1963-1969

	Appearances	Goals
League	153 (4)	25
FA Cup	18	3
League Cup	2	0
Europe	4	3
Other	31 (3)	12
TOTAL	215	

Jimmy was born in Cardonald in Scotland on 17 December 1944. He arrived at White Hart Lane in March 1964 after short spells with Middlesbrough, Celtic and Cowdenbeath, where he was in their senior team when only sixteen. Jimmy gained a Scotland Youth cap and an amateur Scotland cap before he signed as a professional at St Mirren. A place in the Scotland Under-23s against Wales came just three months before Spurs came to call, and after arriving at White Hart Lane for a fee of £25,000 he went straight into the Tottenham team for his debut versus Liverpool at Anfield.

Spurs possessed three wingers for two places at that time and, to accommodate Robertson, Cliff Jones moved to inside forward, with Terry Dyson on the left flank. Later Jimmy became better known at Spurs as a fleet of foot winger who supplied the crosses for Gilzean and Greaves to convert into goals, and for sometimes cutting inside to use his speed to attack the opposition goal himself. He was soon selected for the Scotland team and played against Wales, strangely his solitary appearance for his country at senior level. However he went on to add four more Scotland Under-23 caps to his collection.

Although mainly a right winger, he was not averse to playing on the opposite wing and was an important member of the Tottenham Hotspur FA Cup winning side of 1967, scoring the opening Spurs goal in their 2-1 win over fellow London club Chelsea. The 1966/67 season was Jimmy's best for Tottenham as he missed just 1 match out of the 51 played. Another goal to savour was a crashing volley against Manchester United in their 5-1 defeat at White Hart Lane in October 1965.

Fans were amazed when he moved to rivals Arsenal in 1968, in part exchange for David Jenkins, one of a very few poor decisions by Bill Nicholson. He stayed just two years at Highbury before transferring to Ipswich Town. Jenkins meanwhile was a complete failure at Tottenham, playing only 15 games and appearing mainly in the reserves. Robertson had another two seasons in East Anglia before heading to Stoke City and from there to America, and Seattle Sounders, for one summer. He ended with spells at Walsall and Crewe Alexandra. For Spurs he scored 43 goals in 215 appearances.

Arthur Rowe
Centre half 1930-1938

	Appearances	Goals
League	182	0
FA Cup	19	0
Other	9	0
TOTAL	210	

Arthur Rowe is one of seven Tottenham players to have later returned to manage the club, and he guided Spurs through one of their glorious spells which saw them successful in cup and League. It seems that once a Tottenham man, always a Tottenham man, and throughout the years many former players arrived back at White Hart Lane in some sort of post within the club. Arthur Rowe still remains in the long-time Tottenham supporter's memory as playing an important part in the history of Tottenham Hotspur Football Club. He took a very simple idea and moulded it into a style of play, which was christened 'push and run', which called for first-time passing and allowing the opposition no time to get in their tackles. This idea could be seen as the simple way of the football game before more basic tactics were left behind and complicated systems brought to the forefront. Some pointed to the young boys who, kicking about with a tennis ball in the back yard with their pals, used the brick wall to hit the ball against to make it rebound back to them. All that Spurs managers from 1949 until 1955 did was substitute a player for the wall, and there you had the Tottenham way of playing in the early 1950s.

Arthur Rowe was a Tottenham man through and through, and another true home-grown player, born within a stone's throw of the White Hart Lane stadium. He saw the light of day on 1 September 1906 and played his first competitive football for his school, progressing to the Tottenham Schools team. Acknowledging that the young Rowe was one to keep an eye on, he was connected to Tottenham while still at school. He was soon selected for the London Schools team just three months before he stepped up another rung of the football ladder: move to White Hart Lane as an apprentice in 1923. He narrowly missed an England Schoolboy cap through injury, and then Spurs' nursery clubs Cheshunt and Northfleet played their part in his build-up to the professional ranks in May 1929.

Arthur's first-team debut came in a London FA Charity Cup game against Chelsea in 1930, but he had to wait close to a year before making his first Football League appearance for

Manager Arthur Rowe talks tactics with his 1949/50 Tottenham team.

Spurs versus Burnley on 10 October 1931. He established himself as first choice in the centre half position from then on. Rowe was not a 'stopper' type of defender, but proved he had quite a lot of the skills of the game as well and was a member of an elite club of deep-thinking defenders. As captain of the side he helped Spurs gain promotion to the First Division in 1933, and to third spot the following season. His talent was recognised with a place in the England team against France in December 1933, a match which was played at White Hart Lane, but strangely this was to be his solitary cap for his country. Just after this a bad injury laid him low for almost a year, and Tottenham slid back into the Second Division when he was absent; but when he came back he was never the same.

As his appearances became fewer he decided it was time to retire, and he went to Budapest in Hungary as a coach, but this was soon ended when the Second World War broke out. As a PT instructor he was put in charge of an army team during the conflict, and he took over as manager of Chelmsford City in 1945, moving to Spurs in May 1949. Tottenham had one of their best spells under Rowe, which included the championships of the Second Division and First Division in successive years, 1950 and 1951. He gave his all for Spurs before ill health forced him to step down as manager of Spurs in 1954. He became chief scout for West Bromwich Albion, then manager at Crystal Palace, winding down his career amongst the backroom staff at London clubs Orient and Millwall. He held coaching positions with other London clubs before giving up the game. His appearances for Spurs totalled 210 and he never scored in these.

Frank Saul
Forward 1959-1968

	Appearances	Goals
League	112 (4)	37
FA Cup	7	6
League Cup	1	0
Europe	5	2
Other	33 (4)	15
TOTAL	166	

Born in Canvey Island, Essex, on 23 August 1943, Saul was a youngster who progressed through the Tottenham Hotspur system and could have been the original 'boy wonder'. He played in Spurs' reserves at just fifteen, and appeared in a Tottenham friendly against Crystal Palace in May 1960, scoring a goal. He went on to play his first senior match on 7 September 1960 versus Bolton Wanderers when only seventeen. In that 'double' season of 1960/61 Saul made six appearances at centre forward, as a deputy for Bobby Smith when he was out with an injury, and scored three goals. He was a regular member of the England Youth side at that time. Frank was also a member of the Spurs' successful 1967 FA Cup team at outside left, and scored the second, and winning, Tottenham goal; he had also notched the winner in the semi-final against Nottingham Forest at Hillsborough, Sheffield.

At eighteen he showed what could be the future when scoring twice in the away leg of the European Cup match at Feyenoord, showing much maturity for his years. Being versatile,

he often played on either wing, but his only drawback was that he was not quite consistent enough. When Bobby Smith moved to Brighton in 1964, Saul was handed his chance to show what he was made of; he failed to take the opportunity, although he did score a hat-trick in a 4-1 win over Burnley. Gilzean's arrival at White Hart Lane saw Saul battling to keep his centre forward spot in the team. Probably his best spell came in the 1965/66 season, when he had an extended run while Greaves was absent with hepatitis, and he ended that season by playing for Young England against England in the traditional match on the eve of the cup final.

Having filled in all over the Spurs forward line, Saul moved to Southampton after not quite fulfilling his early promise. He was part of the deal which brought Martin Chivers to Tottenham Hotspur in 1968. He was at the Dell for two years, followed by the same amount of time with Queens Park Rangers, and ended his senior career with five seasons at Millwall. He had a short spell at Dagenham before retiring into business.

	Appearances	Goals
League	229	65
FA Cup	25	12
Other	30	7
TOTAL	284	

One of the great legends of Tottenham Hotspur past, Jimmy Seed seemed to be a product of the south but he was born in the north-east at Blackhill, County Durham, on 25 March 1895. He was a player who was nearly lost to the game before he had actually played a League match, working down the pits and turning out part-time with his local football team, Whitburn, in the Wearside League. But he showed his early promise and was soon being watched by more senior clubs; it was no surprise when he was given a trial at Sunderland and he joined them just before the First World War. The services laid claim to Jimmy and he was serving his country in the Army; most of his wartime football was in the service teams. He had suffered from a slight gas attack during his military duty, causing Sunderland to leave him out of their plans as they thought he had not recovered enough. Still only twenty-four, it seemed his career was over before it had really started, and Seed moved to the other side of Britain.

In south Wales he played for Mid-Rhondda, and although still officially on Sunderland's books he acquired his own release. His health quickly returned and he was once again turning heads in his football each week. After just seven months with the Welsh side, Tottenham brought him to White Hart Lane in February 1920. Spurs manager Peter McWilliam had been watching a player from the opposing team but ended up signing Jimmy instead. At Tottenham, Seed soon settled down as an integral part of the team as Spurs won the FA Cup in 1921. He was also a goalscorer and notched a hat-trick against Bradford City in the cup run.

A regular in the team for close on eight years, and selected for England four times, he suffered an ankle injury which kept him on the sidelines, and when O'Callaghan took his place, Seed was released in 1927 to join Sheffield Wednesday. In 1931 Seed retired and moved into management at Orient, before taking charge at Charlton Athletic in 1933, a post he held until 1956. His 284 appearances for Spurs brought him 84 goals.

Teddy Sheringham
Striker 1992-1997, 2001-2003

	Appearances	Goals
League	184 (2)	97
FA Cup	20	14
League Cup	21	13
Other	30 (1)	20
TOTAL	277	

Teddy Sheringham was born at Highams Park, in north-east London, on 2 April 1966 and admits he was a Spurs admirer at an early age. His father was a policeman and quite a good footballer himself, and Teddy grew up in a footballing family, honing his skills at an early age with miniature games with his brother in the alleys close to their home. Two other sports attracted Teddy as a youngster, table tennis and tennis, but football was always going to be first. His father had been a centre forward as a young player and that was his son's aim. At Selwyn Primary School every minute outside lessons was taken up in playground matches. Sheringham's elder brother was already in the school team and, although three years younger, Teddy managed to get in the team with him. At seven years of age he was picked in the local Cubs side as an outside left, soon moving to centre forward. In a junior cup final at Walthamstow he scored five in an 8-1 win, when still only ten years old.

Still at school, Teddy went training with Leyton Orient and Crystal Palace but eventually joined Millwall after he impressed in a match against their youth side. He progressed through their system and signed as a professional as soon as he was allowed, making his debut against fellow London team Brentford in the Third Division, but he had to wait for his second match before opening his senior goalscoring account against Bournemouth. Teddy was then loaned out to Aldershot for a spell in the 1983/84 season before becoming a part of the Millwall team, but only after a period in Sweden to gain experience. A change of manager gave Teddy his chance, which he took, and it was in 1990/91 that he had his best season at the Den, when he topped the scoring list with 33 League goals, which included four hat-tricks. In 1987/88 Millwall reached the First Division for the first time in their history, but this lasted only two seasons. Sheringham had three of football's top managers during his career: Brian Clough, Terry Venables and Alex Ferguson. At Millwall he netted just under 100 goals in his 220 matches.

Other clubs then took notice and in the summer of 1991 he joined Nottingham Forest for £2 million but, although he scored 21 goals in his first season in the midlands, he was not

Teddy Sheringham doing what he did best, causing panic in the opponents' defence. This header was against Wimbledon.

a real success away from his London roots. Just two games into the next season he returned to the capital, joining Tottenham Hotspur for £2.1 million. He ended his first season at White Hart Lane with 29 goals, winning the Golden Boot award in the Premier League. He also received a call-up for the England squad.

It was always said that Sheringham lacked pace but he more than made up for that with a thinking approach to the game. Amongst his other attributes he had a hard shot and was also unselfish and brave, as a striker in modern-day football has to be. His first spell at White Hart Lane lasted for five years, and he made his Spurs debut against Ipswich Town at Portman Road in a 1-1 draw. In Teddy's second season with Tottenham he was joined in the striker's role by top German scorer Jurgen Klinsmann. Jurgen and Teddy brought the best out of each other

but, in spite of a fairly successful campaign, Klinsmann moved on after just one season. After being named as a substitute for England versus Holland in 1993, he was in the starting line-up for the next game against Poland. Sheringham was not a regular for England at first, but under Terry Venables and then Glenn Hoddle he held down a place in the national side for some years.

Although he was happy at Spurs, Teddy was tempted when Manchester United wanted him to move to Old Trafford, and the move was made ready for the 1997/98 season. Four years later Sheringham returned to Spurs as captain for his second spell, which lasted two years, before he was released and went to Portsmouth for one season; he then joined West Ham United. He scored 144 goals in his 258 appearances for Tottenham.

Bert Smith
Wing half 1916-1929

	Appearances	Goals
League	291	9
FA Cup	28	1
Wartime	7	1
Other	42	2
TOTAL	368	

Bert Smith was born at Higham, near Chatham, in Kent, on 7 March 1892 and much of his early football was learned in south London. Amongst his early clubs were Vanbrugh Park, Crawford United and Metrogas, all in Kent. He seemed to be overlooked by teams in London and the south of England. Yorkshire club Huddersfield Town were the first to notice Smith's capabilities and he joined them in April 1913 as a professional; playing mainly in their reserves, he scored 26 goals in his first season. Then came the First World War and he was called up. He played service football for the army, including one match for the British Army against the French Army.

He often played alongside Bert Bliss and this was to his benefit when he joined Tottenham Hotspur after the war. Smith was an inside forward in those early days and quite a good goalscorer. He had already played for Tottenham during the war as a guest outside left, making his first appearance on 2 December 1916 against Arsenal in the London Combination, the game being at Highbury, where Spurs played many of their home matches during wartime. He also played seven games in 1918/19. When Tottenham acquired his services in 1919 he was switched to right half and took to the change as if he was born to it; he was an instantaneous success.

His first match as a proper Spurs player was on 30 August 1919 versus Coventry City away. He was part of the successful Spurs side to win the Second Division Championship and the FA Cup in the first two seasons after the war. He had a reputation as a hard-tackling player, and he was certainly a strong and virile competitor, always full of energy. Bert was a first choice for the eight years he was at White Hart Lane, and after two international trial games he made his England debut against Scotland in April 1921, appearing with three other Spurs, Grimsdell, Bliss and Dimmock. He only appeared for England on two other occasions.

In May 1930 he became a coach at Northfleet and then at Sheppey United, before going to Berne, Switzerland as a player-coach. He also worked with Stevenage and Harwich before moving to Hitchin where he became their groundsman, until retiring in 1966. Many of the items he gathered while playing were the basis of a museum in Hitchin's ground for many years; I wonder where those all went to? He made 368 appearances for Spurs, scoring 13 goals.

Bobby Smith

Centre forward 1955-1964

	Appearances	Goals
League	271	176
FA Cup	32	22
Europe	14	10
Other	41 (1)	43
TOTAL	359	

For nine years Bobby Smith led the Tottenham Hotspur attack with dash and energy, taking all the knocks that went with his style of play. He was born in Lingdale in North Yorkshire on 22 February 1933, the son of a miner, and showed all his native grit throughout his career. His job was scoring goals, and that he did with relish, in turn intimidating defenders and especially goalkeepers. Bobby started out as a youngster with Redcar Boys Club, Tudor Rose and Redcar United before he joined Chelsea in 1948, as an amateur, turning professional in 1950. He impressed so much at Stamford Bridge that he was in the Chelsea League team at the age of seventeen, and notched 30 goals in 86 games.

Spurs came in to sign him for £16,000 in December 1955, and he quickly made his debut on 24 December 1955 against Luton Town. The North London side were struggling near the foot of the League table, but Smith scored the goals that saved Spurs from relegation that season and became a legendary Spurs figure from then onwards, taking over the centre forward spot from the long-serving Duquemin. He scored 30 goals or more in each season from 1957/58, when he had 38, up to the 'double' season of 1961, when he weighed in with 33. He also netted in both Tottenham FA Cup successes in 1961 and 1962. England could not ignore the bustling centre forward and he won his first cap for his country against Northern Ireland in October 1960; he went on to score 13 goals in 15 appearances. He showed sheer artistry in his precise chip over the Spanish goalkeeper at Wembley in 1960, while another performance to remember came with a hat-trick against Manchester United at Old Trafford in a 4-3 victory. Bobby also had a short spell as Tottenham captain before Danny Blanchflower arrived.

After years of tussles with enthusiastic defenders he began to slow down, and in May 1964 he joined Brighton for just £5,000, where he began to score freely again to help the South Coast team win the Fourth Division title. This was his only season there, however, and he moved just along the coast to Hastings in October 1965, finally finishing his playing days with a short spell at Banbury United. He scored 251 goals for Spurs in his 359 appearances.

Robert Steele
Inside forward 1908-1916

	Appearances	Goals
League	230	41
FA Cup	19	5
Wartime	30	6
Other	37	10
TOTAL	316	

Robert was the youngest of the three Steele brothers who were at White Hart Lane together but only appeared once in the same team, this being against Bradford City at White Hart Lane on 29 January 1910. In fact, this was the only game in which Alex Steele played for the seniors. Robert was born at Newmilns in Ayrshire, Scotland, on 25 June 1888, and throughout his early career he alternated between centre half and inside forward, but on joining Tottenham he settled in at inside left. After appearing for his home town, he also played for Kilwinning, and then Port Glasgow, before he came south to White Hart Lane in May 1908, just in time to make his debut against Wolverhampton Wanderers on 1 August 1908, Spurs' first match in the Football League.

Robert missed just one Spurs game, League and cup, in their first season with the big boys, and helped them to promotion to the First Division at the first attempt, scoring 14 goals in the process. During the early days of Tottenham in the Football League he could be relied upon to score his fair share of goals, but the nearest he came to playing for his country was a trial match in March 1909 between home-based Scots and the Scotland players who had moved south. At this time there was a marked reluctance to select Anglo-Scots for international honours. Robert was one of a few players in this period who could put in a good performance in the passing game or, if it were more appropriate, take the ball into the opponents' goalmouth with a clever dribble. When his brother Daniel left Spurs, Robert moved from inside left to take his place at centre half, and when the First World War came along he showed how he could play in other positions: left-back, outside left, left half and centre forward.

The 1915/16 season was his last for Spurs, making 30 appearances and scoring 6 goals; his last appearance was on 29 April 1916. After the war he was released and became a referee, mainly in the Southern League. He was persuaded to play for Gillingham for a short spell until retiring altogether to take up more leisurely sports; he captained the England bowls team. His 316 Spurs appearances produced 62 goals.

Sandy Tate
Full-back 1899-1908

	Appearances	Goals
S. League	207	3
W. League	79	2
FA Cup	36	0
London League	15	1
South District Cup	14	0
Other	71	6
TOTAL	422	

Sandy Tate was one of the most feared of Tottenham Hotspur defenders, spending nine years at White Hart Lane from 1899 to 1908. He played most of his games in the Southern League and at that time Spurs were playing in two different leagues, the Western League being the other main competition. In fact, in the 1903/04 season Spurs played 70 matches, calling on thirty-three players, and Tate played in 50 of these. Sandy was born in Glenbuck in Ayrshire, Scotland, in 1873, and as one of thirteen children he had to do his bit for the family budget, so he worked as a pit boy, combining this with playing football for Glenbuck Athletic. He then had a short spell with Ayr and then Royal Albert for three years, during which time he played as an amateur for top Scottish club Rangers. At the age of nineteen Sandy turned professional with Motherwell; he then caught the eye of Preston North End and moved south to Lancashire.

He came to the new Tottenham ground at White Hart Lane in May 1899 and went straight into the team against Millwall Athletic on 2 September 1899, playing in all the Southern League games in his first season. Spurs won the League that season and journeyed to such exotic places as Cowes, Bedminster and Chatham. With his ferocity in tackling, Tate was an important player in the Tottenham FA Cup-winning side of 1901. Although he looked ferocious, he was really a very fair-minded defender, who more than made up for his slow pace with his speed of thought, and throughout his Spurs career he was never once booked, which says it all. He was a constant performer for Spurs and was reckoned to be the best left-back in the country, giving Tottenham remarkable service, and taking on the captaincy when J.L. Jones left the club in 1904. Tate, despite his regular top-class performances, was overlooked by his country; the nearest he got was in March 1903, in a Scottish international trial match.

His Spurs days came to an end when he moved to Leyton in May 1908, where he was later manager, before filling the same post at Croydon Common for two years. After a period away from the game he reappeared as coach to the famous Corinthians in 1922. His appearances for Tottenham numbered 422 and he scored 12 goals.

Peter Taylor
Winger 1976-1980

	Appearances	Goals
League	116 (7)	31
FA Cup	8 (3)	2
League Cup	4 (2)	0
Other	27 (6)	13
TOTAL	173	

Peter Taylor is one of the Tottenham Hotspur players who went on to be manager of the England team, albeit only for a short spell as acting manager while the FA dithered. He later took charge of the England Under-21 side. He was born in Rochford, in Essex, on 3 January 1953 and was soon selected for Canvey Island and then South East Essex Schoolboys. He was on Spurs' books as a youngster but was rejected when he failed to impress, so he joined Southend as an apprentice and attained professional status in January 1971.

At Southend he stood out as someone who had great potential and Crystal Palace signed him in October 1973. His performances at Selhurst Park soon saw him playing for the England Under-23 side, gaining four caps. Peter was a talented goal-scoring winger and he became one of a small band of Third Division players who played for England, his first match coming against Wales in March 1976, when he made a goalscoring debut; he quickly made three further appearances.

He moved to Tottenham for £400,000 in September 1976 and appeared in the Spurs' white shirt at West Bromwich Albion for his first match; although he scored a goal Spurs lost 4-2. Taylor was a fast raiding winger who was not afraid to do his stint in defence, but despite being second in the Spurs' scoring list with eight goals, he could not prevent them from sliding into the Second Division that season. Missing just one match the next season, Peter weighed in with 12 goals as Tottenham rebounded straight back into the First Division.

When the two Argentine stars arrived at White Hart Lane, Taylor was one player who found himself sometimes overlooked, and after only a few appearances in the first team, he was allowed to join Orient in 1980, from where he went to Oldham. Injuries slowed him down and, after spells at Maidstone and Exeter City, he dropped into non-League football as manager at Heybridge Swifts, Chelmsford City, Dartford and Enfield. He came back into the League as Steve Perryman's assistant at Watford, later taking the manager's post with Leicester City. He was manager at Hull City, with some success, and is back in charge of England Under-21s. He returned to League management with Crystal Palace. His 46 goals for Spurs came in 173 appearances.

Erik Thorstvedt
Goalkeeper 1988-1994

	Appearances	Goals
League	171 (2)	0
FA Cup	14	0
League Cup	25	0
Europe	6	0
Other	11 (3)	0
TOTAL	232	

Norway's international goalkeeper could well have been lost to Tottenham Hotspur after having a trial period in December 1984, as circumstances meant he went home after two outings in the reserve side. But he returned four years later and this time he stayed. Born in Stavanger in Norway on 28 October 1962, Thorstvedt began his career with EIK and Viking Stavanger in Norway, and had a trial period in Germany with Borussia Moenchengladbach after his short spell in England. He then joined Swedish club IFK Gothenburg, and with Spurs having a problem with goalkeepers he was signed by manager Terry Venables for £400,000 in December 1988.

Erik, at 6ft 4in, became a cult figure at White Hart Lane, even after making his debut in a televised match versus Nottingham Forest on 15 January 1989, when he made a mistake to give Forest the winning goal. After this early setback he took time to find his way in English football and he faced competition for the Spurs goalkeeping position from the young Ian Walker, each having quite long spells in the senior Tottenham Hotspur side. Aptly dubbed 'Erik

the Viking' by the Spurs supporters, he was a seasoned international with 51 caps for Norway when he arrived at White Hart Lane.

He was a 'stopper' first and foremost, rather than a goalkeeper who commanded the penalty area, but he soon became first choice and guarded the Spurs goal against all comers for the next five years. His bulky frame was often seen as filling the whole goal by opposing strikers and, as with Pat Jennings some years earlier, Erik made many vital saves with his legs and other parts of his body, proving a good goalkeeper has to put anything in the way to stop sides scoring. His style of play seemed quite casual at times and although he had the height advantage, plus seemingly long arms, he was sometimes at fault at crosses, but he worked on this. He won an FA Cup winners medal in 1991 against Nottingham Forest, becoming one of the Spurs goalkeepers who stayed fixed in Tottenham fans' memories. A fractured finger in 1993 proved troublesome for a while and his Spurs career ended in 1994 after 232 appearances. He went on to coach Norway's national XI.

	Appearances	Goals
League	96	0
FA Cup	6	0
Wartime	36	0
Other	13	0
TOTAL	151	

A strong and determined defender who, with many other youngsters, had his early footballing years interrupted by the Second World War, being sixteen when the conflict began. Born in Stepney, in east London, on 10 April 1923, Tickridge was a product of the fine Spurs youth policy of the 1930s, and after playing for his district and England Schools he started his Spurs career with Tottenham Juniors. He joined the ground staff in 1937 and played for the Spurs nursery club Northfleet, and then for Dartford during 1940/41.

He made his Tottenham debut on 30 August 1941 against Watford in the London War League and went on to play in every game of the 1941/42 season. He was then called up for the Royal Navy, which limited his football to service games, although he did play as a guest for Millwall, Fulham and Crystal Palace. After four years in the Navy, playing as an amateur throughout the war years, Tickridge signed professional forms for Spurs in 1946 having played for the reformed Tottenham reserves. He made his first Football League appearance for Spurs at home to Southampton on 9 September 1946, and played in 14 matches that season after

taking the place of Arthur Willis, who then found it hard to displace the younger player. Tickridge went on to miss just four games in the following two seasons. He proved himself a very reliable full-back, at home in either of the two positions, and in his early twenties looked ripe for a long career at White Hart Lane.

This was until the arrival of Alf Ramsey from Southampton in May 1949, which resulted in Sid's appearances becoming few and far between. Indeed, he only played two more games for Spurs in their glory years of the Second and First Division Championships. He left Tottenham to go to Chelsea in March 1951. He later moved on to Brentford for eighteen months, until injury decided his football playing days were over, and he retired early in 1957. He became assistant trainer at Millwall until he returned to White Hart Lane as the youth team manager. He made 151 appearances for Tottenham but never managed to score a goal.

Ricardo Villa
Midfield 1978-1988

	Appearances	Goals
League	123 (9)	18
FA Cup	21	3
League Cup	15 (1)	3
Europe	8 (1)	1
Other	43 (2)	16
TOTAL	223	

Ricardo Villa is remembered by all Tottenham supporters as the scorer of one of the great goals, which won the FA Cup for Spurs in 1981 against Manchester City. This was in the replay after the two teams had fought out a draw at Wembley, with Villa being substituted and trudging off to the dressing room with head bowed. Born in Buenos Aires, in Argentina, on 10 April 1952, he first played for two lesser known Argentine clubs, Quilmes and Atletico Tucuman, before moving up to Racing Club Buenos Aires as the most costly player at that time. Although he had appeared in his country's winning World Cup team of 1978, he was little known elsewhere.

He joined Tottenham with his fellow Argentinian, Ossie Ardiles, the following summer, and made his competitive Spurs debut at Nottingham Forest on 19 August 1978. He scored Spurs' goal in the 1-1 draw in Nottingham, although he had appeared in a pre-season friendly against Royal Antwerp in Belgium. Villa was a strong running midfielder who liked to link up in attack, shown by his total of 41 goals in his 223 appearances for Tottenham. He also played for his country on 18 occasions. Villa's relaxed way of playing led to the fans thinking he was not really interested in what was going on around him, but it disguised the serious way he approached his football. He was quite different in training and enjoyed a good laugh with his fellow players. He was valued at £375,000 in the double transfer which brought him and Ardiles to White Hart Lane, and at first he lived next door to his friend Ossie.

Ricky was never what you could call a regular in the early 1980s, often being on the substitutes' bench as his form dipped and rose alarmingly. It was sometimes said that to get a return pass from the bearded South American, the other players had to go and get it from him. It was during the Falklands conflict that he faltered, as opposing fans gave him rather a tough time. He left Spurs in 1983 to play in the United States for Fort Lauderdale Strikers, before returning to South America and Deportivo Cali of Colombia. Going home to Argentina, Villa assisted Defensa Y Justicia, and also coached them.

	Appearances	Goals
League	137 (1)	33
FA Cup	14	5
League Cup	21	4
Other	40 (4)	12
TOTAL	217	

Chris Waddle was another talented player from the north-east, being born in Gateshead on 14 December 1960, although his skills were not realised when he trained with Newcastle United nor when he was an associated schoolboy at Coventry City. He played for local junior teams around his home, including Pelaw Juniors, Whitehouse Club, Mount Pleasant Social Club and Learn Lane Club, before being attracted to one of the top amateur clubs in his area, Tow Law Town, in 1978. From there he had an unsuccessful trial period at Sunderland, but Newcastle United took him aboard in July 1980. He made rapid progress at St James' Park and by October 1980 he had made his debut, and alongside players such as Peter Beardsley and Kevin Keegan he helped Newcastle gain promotion in 1984. He quickly became their top player and won his first England Under-21 cap in October, against Finland, and a full cap soon followed against Republic of Ireland.

He had already made eight appearances for England when he was brought to White Hart Lane for £650,000 in July 1985. He made his Spurs debut against Watford on 17 August 1985, scoring twice, both headers, in a Tottenham victory. At 6ft tall, Waddle had a hunched-up run which took him swiftly past defenders to set up many goals, and he scored his share as well. Given a licence to play all over the ground, Waddle was showing his intelligent distribution and scintillating ball control to great effect, and also linked up well with Glenn Hoddle in one of the best midfield duos for a long time. The two also got together to record a top hit record entitled 'Diamond Lights', but the less said of that the better. When Hoddle moved abroad, Waddle took over the mantle of midfield maestro to orchestrate Spurs performances.

He gained another 36 England caps while at Tottenham, and although they wanted him to stay, a £4.5 million offer saw him move to Olympique de Marseille, the French champions, in 1989. He returned to home shores in 1992 to play for Sheffield Wednesday, followed by short spells at other clubs. His 217 appearances for Spurs saw him notch 54 goals.

Fred 'Fanny' Walden
Winger 1912-1926

	Appearances	Goals
League	214	21
FA Cup	22	4
Wartime	68	15
Other	20	6
TOTAL	324	

Fred Walden was one of the smallest players to appear for Tottenham Hotspur. In fact, he was one of the smallest footballers ever, standing at just 5ft 2in and weighing 8st 9lbs. A story circulating while he was at White Hart Lane was that he once pushed the ball through an opponent's legs and followed himself. Walden was born in Wellingborough in Northants on 3 May 1888. He appeared for local clubs White Cross, All Saints and Rodwell before being taken aboard by Wellingborough Town. Twisting and dodging his way through matches, he moved to Northampton Town around 1909, and surprisingly made his debut for them in the Southern League at centre forward, where he popped up with a hat-trick. He was soon at his best position on the right wing, where his skills could cause the most danger.

Tottenham paid a record £1,700 to bring him to White Hart Lane and his first match on 19 April 1913 was against Woolwich Arsenal; he had already played in an international trial match the previous month. He sparkled on the Spurs wing and earned his first England cap in April 1914, but then along came the First World War, although he was an ever-present for Spurs in the 1914/15 season. He had one season with Leeds City during the conflict, but with peace once more Walden became one of the brightest stars of the Tottenham Hotspur 1920 promotion team and the FA Cup winning side in 1921. However, he was forced to miss the final itself through an injured knee. Eight years after his first match for England, Walden was selected for the international against Wales in March 1922. In a period when heavy charging was the norm for defenders, he did not suffer much from this, probably because they couldn't get down to his level.

He returned to Northampton for his final season in 1926, retiring in 1927. 'Fanny' Walden was also a fine cricketer for his county, scoring well over 7,000 runs and taking 100 wickets as a bowler. After 258 games for Northants he then became a well-respected umpire. His 324 Spurs games saw him score 46 goals.

Ian Walker
Goalkeeper 1991-2001

	Appearances	Goals
League	257 (2)	0
FA Cup	25	0
League Cup	22 (1)	0
Europe	6	0
Other	74	0
TOTAL	387	

Ian Walker came up through the Spurs ranks to become a first-team regular and an England international. He was born in Watford on 31 October 1971, and as a promising young goalkeeper he had been on the books at Queens Park Rangers as an associated schoolboy. The son of Mike Walker, also a goalkeeper, Ian joined Tottenham as a trainee after graduating at the FA School of Excellence at Lilleshall, and helped the Tottenham youth team win the FA Youth Cup in 1990. He became England's regular goalkeeper from the Under-15s to the Under-19s level. With four other goalkeepers at White Hart Lane, to give him first-team experience, Walker was loaned out to Oxford United, in November, and Ipswich Town, in December, during 1990. Standing at 6ft 1in he made his England Under-21 debut before making his first senior appearance for Spurs. His senior debut for Spurs came towards the end of the 1990/91 season at Norwich, on 10 April 1991, with his father on the Norwich bench as a coach for the Norfolk club. Quick and agile, Walker also showed that he was also able to get down to low shots better than many other tall goalkeepers, and soon flourished under the eye of former Liverpool and Tottenham goalkeeper Ray Clemence. He had several lengthy spells as a regular at White Hart Lane, and for a while kept the Norway international goalkeeper Erik Thorstvedt out of the Spurs First XI. Ian also gained a Football League Cup winners' medal with Tottenham in 1999. Walker left White Hart Lane in 2001 after ten years and over 300 appearances at Spurs, and joined Leicester City. He was still being named in England squads although he was performing in the Coca-Cola Championship and not in the Premier League. He later became reserve keeper at Bolton Wanderers

	Appearances	Goals
War League	7	
TOTAL	7	

Although not a player anymore, John deserves to be named as one of the Tottenham greats, as Spurs have been his life for over fifty years. He was born in Finchley in 1922, and as a youngster played for, and captained, Mill Hill, Hendon and Middlesex and London Schoolboys, joining Spurs' ground staff straight from school as an amateur in 1936, and then signing professional forms in 1938. At the beginning of the 1939/40 season Johnny was with Tottenham Juniors and the 'A' team, but his career was not helped by the Second World War breaking out. Although not the tallest of players, he was a most accomplished full-back and made guest appearances for Enfield during the war; he was noted as one to watch for the future. He was then called upon to make his senior Tottenham debut versus Arsenal away on 23 November 1940, this being at White Hart Lane as Arsenal were sharing the ground during the war. Wallis played three times in 1940/41

and had four games in 1944/45. After joining the Army he was posted abroad with the Royal Artillery and sustained a serious shrapnel wound from a land mine when serving in Palestine. Although he tried a comeback for Spurs, the injury signalled the end of a professional football career with Tottenham. He played some non-League football with Chelmsford City and Wisbech, before joining the Spurs backroom staff in 1948 and studying medical matters and coaching. John took on many different posts within the Tottenham Hotspur club. First he was assistant trainer, and then he took over as the trainer when Bill Nicholson became manager. He was appointed manager of the reserves in 1964 and became the club physiotherapist until 1975 when he was appointed kit manager, a post he held until he retired in 1994 after a lifetime of serving Tottenham Hotspur. He made seven appearances for Spurs, all in the war years, truly a Spurs legend after a lifetime behind the scenes.

Bill 'Sonny' Walters
Winger 1943-1956

	Appearances	Goals
League	211	66
FA Cup	23	5
Wartime	50	14
Other	63	24
TOTAL	347	

A Tottenham Hotspur legend who was a very direct winger, Walters forced defenders on to the back foot when he ran at them with speed. He came to prominence in the war years, making his debut at Fulham on Christmas Day 1943, scoring in the 2-0 victory. After one more full season Walters was called up for the Army, and played most of his service years for the British Army team. He was a regular for the side playing against other European Army sides, as well as the RAF and the Royal Navy. He was the son of a former soccer captain of Haywards Sports FC and was under Spurs' wing as soon as he left school. He appeared as an amateur, aged fourteen, for Tottenham Juniors and was loaned to Walthamstow Avenue and Finchley. He also had one match with Millwall.

Born in Edmonton on 5 September 1924, Walters trod the well-known path to White Hart Lane via Edmonton Schools and London Schools. He became a full professional and made his debut against West Bromwich Albion on 4 January 1947. When Freddie Cox moved to Arsenal, Walters staked his claim for the no.7 shirt and wore it with success and pride. With a hard shot, 'Sonny' was the top scorer when Spurs won the Second Division trophy in

1949/50, and was also a part of the championship side of 1950/51.

Most unfortunate to be playing in the era of Stanley Matthews and Tom Finney, Walters' only England appearance was for England 'B'. Holland in February 1950; he also played for the FA team against the Army at Charlton. There was nothing of the showman about Walters' play, but he was, in his time, one of the most dangerous wingers around. His nickname of 'Sonny' well describes the way in which the speedy winger played, often with a smile on his face. After scoring 109 goals in his 347 appearances for Spurs, he moved to Aldershot in July 1957 for his final two seasons. It was a shock when his death was announced in November 1970 at the early age of forty-six, and the large turnout at his funeral of Tottenham players, past and present, showed how much he was respected at White Hart Lane.

Inside forward 1959-1964

	Appearances	Goals
League	183	40
FA Cup	19	1
Europe	17	6
Other	14	6
TOTAL	233	

On 21 July 1964, when sheltering from a thunderstorm under a tree on the Crews Hill golf course at Enfield, John White was tragically struck down. He was at the peak of his career at the age of twenty-seven and was looked upon by manager Bill Nicholson as the man to build a new Tottenham Hotspur team around. John was born on 28 April 1937 in Musselburgh, Scotland, also the birthplace of Tottenham's Dave Mackay. Junior sides Musselburgh and Bonnyrigg Rose Athletic were the first to parade the talent of the slenderly built White, and he soon attracted the attention of more senior clubs. Alloa Athletic signed him in August 1956, where he stayed for two seasons, before he was transferred to another Scottish outfit, Falkirk, for £3,300 in August 1958. He had been offered to Charlton Athletic while at Alloa, but was thought to be too much of a lightweight. Charlton were not the only ones who thought this way, as Glasgow Rangers and Middlesbrough rejected him as a teenager. Within one year of his move to Falkirk, White was selected for Scotland. West Germany

in May 1959, and in the following September he was in the Scottish League side to face the League of Ireland.

Tottenham brought White to White Hart Lane for £20,000 in October 1959, although the move was held up so that he could play a second match for the Scottish League versus the Irish League. He was put straight into the Spurs team, making his debut in the away game at Sheffield Wednesday on 17 October 1959, and although they lost 2-1, John scored the Spurs goal. He played in three different positions in his first season at Tottenham, including a spell on the right wing. With the nucleus of a great side being gathered, White was in his best position of inside right as the 1960/61 season kicked off, which ended in the League and FA Cup double. Four players played in every match that season, including John White, who also weighed in with 13 goals, although he was not too renowned for his scoring.

His strike rate was above average as he reached double figures in three out of four seasons at

John White thwarted by goalkeeper Gaskell of Manchester United at White Hart Lane.

Spurs, and in Europe he scored with two headers against Rangers and also got a goal in the Cup-Winners' final against Atletico Madrid. Together with his captain, Danny Blanchflower, he ran the midfield of the Spurs machine. The following season saw White miss just six games as Tottenham finished third in the League and took the FA Cup to White Hart Lane for the second year. John soon acquired the nickname of 'The Ghost' from the Spurs supporters, as he would suddenly appear in the right position at the right time during matches, popping up in plenty of space to make use of this to the best advantage. For such a slightly built player the midfield position was thought to be too crowded for White, but with great vision and control he always seemed to have plenty of time to control the ball and it was laid off nearly every time to a teammate. He also had the stamina to play through the wet and muddy White Hart Lane, which was never like the pure surface the pitch is nowadays.

Some called him the second Tommy Harmer, but he was certainly the first and only John White, as their talents were different. Harmer's ball control and trickery were his game; White was the one who could pinpoint his passes, long and short, to do the most effective damage to the Spurs' opponents. During his time with Tottenham Hotspur, he gained 18 full caps for Scotland plus one for the Scotland Under-23s. John White made 233 appearances for Spurs and scored 53 goals.

Arthur Willis
Full-back 1942-1954

	Appearances	Goals
League	145	1
FA Cup	16	0
Wartime	73	0
Other	39	1
TOTAL	273	

Born at Denaby Main in Northumberland on 2 February 1920, Arthur was a noted schoolboy player, but he was working as a miner and playing football whenever he could when he was spotted by three clubs. He chose Tottenham Hotspur, the southernmost club, over Barnsley and Sunderland. Signing amateur forms for Spurs in 1938, he was promptly loaned out to Northfleet to polish up his skills. During the war he worked in an engineering factory and played for Finchley.

He made his Spurs debut during the war against Charlton Athletic on 24 April 1943, his only game that season, but went on to play regularly for the remainder of the war, making 81 appearances. He also played once as a guest during this time for Millwall. Willis continued to be a regular for Tottenham in the years immediately following, although there were two other contenders for his position. After losing his place to Withers in the 1950 promotion-winning Spurs team, he regained his left-back spot the next season when Tottenham Hotspur won the First Division Championship. His form during this season also earned him an international cap for England versus France, which was his only appearance for his country. His solitary League goal came on 14 March 1953 when he scored a penalty against Chelsea; the regular Tottenham spot-kick expert, Alf Ramsey, was not playing. The only other goal that Willis recorded was also a penalty in the tour match against Hanover Arminia of Germany on 14 May 1950.

Arthur Willis left Tottenham to join his former Spurs captain Ron Burgess at Swansea Town in 1954. He played in South Wales for four years, which included a Welsh Cup final in 1956. After being on the coaching staff at Swansea he took over as player-manager for Haverfordwest in the Welsh League. Willis made 273 appearances and scored 2 goals for Tottenham.

	Appearances	Goals
S. League	105	45
W. League	15	7
FA Cup	24	5
League	27	18
Wartime	1	0
Other	25	25
TOTAL	197	

Vivian Woodward was an amateur centre forward and an architect who more than held his own in the top flight of football. He joined Tottenham Hotspur in 1900; his first game was against Bristol City in the Southern League in April of the following year. He was limited in his appearances at first, owing to his work, playing twice, and it was the same the following season with just three matches. Woodward was born in South London in 1879 and, when at Ascham College in Clacton, he started playing football with Clacton and Harwich & Parkeston. He stood out as an elegant player, standing nearly six feet tall, who relied on pure skill in an era when hard running and brawn were at the forefront.

He joined the ranks of Chelmsford City where he began scoring goals on a regular basis, and by 1903 he was turning out for Tottenham. He registered hat-tricks twice in that season; the first in a 7-0 victory against Brighton, and then against Reading in a high-scoring 7-4 win. In 1903 Woodward was selected for the full England side and he scored twice against Ireland. He registered 28 goals in 23 appearances, and was an automatic choice for the England Amateurs with 53 goals in 38 games.

When Spurs were elected into the Football League, Woodward was one of the scorers in the first match, which they won 3-0 against Wolverhampton Wanderers on 1 September 1908, and he helped Spurs gain promotion in their first season. He was still turning out for former club Chelmsford as well as Spurs, as well as playing in various other matches, including a North v. South amateur trial, for which he claimed just 6d for expenses. As a pure amateur Woodward gained two Olympic gold medals with Great Britain, in 1908 and 1912, when he appeared at outside left. Added to this, he played in many matches abroad with various teams.

He was a fine ambassador for British soccer with trips to Hungary, Austria and Bohemia in 1908, and a tour to South Africa as captain of the famous Corinthians, coupled with a tour of the United States with the 'Pilgrims'. He was an all-round sportsman, shining at cricket. In the summer of 1909 he decided to retire, but to Spurs' surprise he made a quick return in Chelsea's colours in the following November. He served as a director for both Spurs and Chelsea while a player. He passed away in January 1954.

Other titles published by Stadia

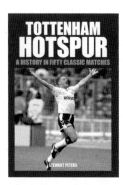

Tottenham Hotspur A History in Fifty Classic Matches
STEWART PETERS

For over 120 years Tottenham Hotspur have scaled the heights of English and European football. This book captures the fifty classic matches that best epitomise the achievements, players and history of the legendary Spurs. From the early days of FA Cup glory at Burnden Park in 1901 to the lifting of the Worthington Cup at Wembley in 1999 and beyond, all of the great moments are here.

0 7524 3612 0

Tottenham Hotspur FC 1882-1952
ROY BRAZIER

This book of over 200 images celebrates the first seven decades in the history of the remarkable Tottenham Hotspur Football Club. The selection includes action shots, programmes, cartoons, team groups and other items of significant memorabilia that evoke the rich football heritage of the famous north London outfit. Essential reading for anyone with an interest in the club, this book gives an evocative glimpse into the history of one of the most glamorous clubs to play the beautiful game.

0 7524 2044 5

Gravesend & Northfleet FC
PAUL HARRISON

This book documents the sixty-year history of Gravesend & Northfleet Football Club. It explores, for the first time, the stories of Northfleet United and Gravesend United, the original clubs who remained separate for so long, paying particular attention to the connection with the mighty Tottenham Hotspur that saw so many future stars turn out for the Fleet. This book allows the reader to look back at the players and matches of yesteryear and also provides a lasting record of the club as it is today.

0 7524 3795 X

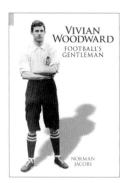

Vivian Woodward Football's Gentleman
NORMAN JACOBS

One of the true greats of English football, Vivian Woodward led England to victory in both the 1908 and 1912 Olympic Games. Having signed for Tottenham Hotspur in 1901, he scored Spurs' first goal in League football and went on to become the best-known name in the sport. He played in more than 60 internationals and was credited with scoring eight goals in a 15-0 drubbing of France in Paris! Woodward's biography will appeal to anyone with an interest in the history of English football.

0 7524 3430 6

If you are interested in purchasing other books published by Stadia, or in case you have difficulty finding any Stadia books in your local bookshop, you can also place orders directly through the Tempus Publishing website

www.tempus-publishing.com